Hollywood Cheesecake

Hollywood Cheesecake

*Celebrating a century of love and devotion
to the photogenic wonders of
the prettiest girls with the prettiest legs
in the most glamorous profession of 'em all—
show business.*

by Madison S. Lacy
and Don Morgan

THE CITADEL PRESS   SECAUCUS, NEW JERSEY

ACKNOWLEDGMENTS

No book on the subject of leg art could be compiled by one person without generous help supplied by others. The photos contained herein—many of them great collector's items today—were brought to light over a period of several years. Some came from old boxes and crates stored beneath sound stages and almost forgotten. They emerged from attics, trunks, old filing cabinets, and of course, treasured personal collections. Others were purchased from various bookstores, large and small.

For their blessed efforts and cooperation, I am extremely grateful and deeply indebted to such film companies as Columbia, Metro-Goldwyn-Mayer, Paramount, 20th Century-Fox, United Artists, Samuel Goldwyn, American International, First National, Warner Bros., and Universal; such broadcasting companies as CBS, NBC, and ABC; many smaller production units that no longer exist; and such individuals as Anne Schlosser of the American Film Institute, Mildred Simpson of the Academy of Motion Picture Arts and Sciences Library, Diane Goodrich, Gene Ringgold (for his sage advice as well as his great photo collection), Dion McGregor and Mort Lichter, Sylvia Rabin, and Jack Kingsley of the Warner Bros. still department. And special thanks to John Kobal of England for smoking out some of the hard-to-find leg art among these pages.

First paperbound printing

Copyright © 1981 by Don Morgan & Lois Lacy
All rights reserved
Published by Citadel Press
A division of Lyle Stuart Inc.
120 Enterprise Ave., Secaucus, N.J. 07094
In Canada: Musson Book Company
A division of General Publishing Co. Limited
Don Mills, Ontario
Manufactured in the United States of America by
Halliday Lithograph, West Hanover, Mass.
Designed by A. Christopher Simon

Library of Congress Cataloging in Publication Data

Lacy, Madison S.
    Leg art.

    1. Glamour photography.   2. Lacy, Madison S.
I. Morgan, Don.   II. Title.
TR678.L32   770'.92'4 [B]   81-1868
                                                  AACR2

ISBN 0-8065-0830-2 (pbk.)

This book was originally published under the title LEG ART

CONTENTS

REQUIEM

AUTHOR'S NOTE

FOREWORD BY James Cagney

INTRODUCTION   11

LEG ART—Its early days from Mythology
to Mazepa.   33

THE DAY THAT LEG MET ART   41

THE BIG SHOW IN SHOW BIZ   47

THE VANITY FAIR MAIDS   53

THE NAME IS THE FAME OF THE
GAME—From the Naked Lady and the
Biograph Girl to Oomph and Ping   57

. . . AND OTHER LEG ART LADIES   73

A GALLERY OF LEG ART LADIES   81

INDEX   283

REQUIEM

As I told his wife, Lois, during those first emotional shock waves that inevitably follow word of the demise of a close and treasured friend, Madison Lacy departed this earth in much the same manner that he had always wrapped up his motion-picture photo assignments. Everything in its proper place, no chores left undone, no excuses, no apologies. The job was completed, it had been executed perfectly, and it was time to move along to a new challenge.

During the final, painful months of enduring a terminal illness, Maddy never for a moment ceased his efforts to bring to print his panegyric in honor of the pulchritudinous pinions displayed by famous ladies of show business. *Leg Art* was a self-appointed task that Maddy was determined to complete before he moved on to something else.

We had been close friends and working associates for three decades, and I was honored when he asked for my assistance. It was a privilege to contribute in some small way to the creation of *Leg Art*. But make no mistake—*Leg Art* is Madison Lacy's book. I was merely a collaborator, luxuriating in his wondrous reminiscences, enthralled by his vast collection of memorable photos, titillated by his bottomless store of memorabilia.

Today, as *Leg Art* arrives at the bookstalls, I am enjoying the first months of retirement, having terminated forty-five years as a motion-picture publicist. I have already begun to compile my own memoirs, which are concentrated on the hilarity and humor of Hollywood that combined to make the movie capital the craziest, most mixed-up, fun-loving, unpredictable community in the world.

My life in films had begun at Fox before it merged with 20th Century. My earliest associations were with such stars as Will Rogers, Tyrone Power, Shirley Temple, Jane Withers, and Alice Faye. I was fortunate enough to work on such box-office hits as *Imitation of Life, The Glenn Miller Story, Thoroughly Modern Millie, Airport,* and *The Towering Inferno.* My final effort as a unit publicist was at MGM with Marlon Brando and George C. Scott in *The Formula.*

It's a lifetime I wouldn't exchange with those of kings and presidents.

I know that Madison Lacy felt the same as I do. After all, Maddy *was* Hollywood, beginning with D. W. Griffith and riding the movieland merry-go-round every single day of his earthly presence.

We are all lucky, indeed, that we have become benefactors of a Lacy legacy that has bequeathed to us the nostalgic charm of his life-long love affair with leg art.

DON MORGAN

AUTHOR'S NOTE

It is with a generous portion of sadness and frustration that I must notify readers that the great and talented photographers whose accomplishments are contained within these pages must go unrecognized.

The motion-picture industry is the culprit. Down through the years the still photographers who covered film sets, photographing the scenes, the stars, and the filmmakers, were forced to perform in anonymity. Their names did not appear on the screen credits or on the photos they captured. With the exception of a rare few portrait photographers, they existed in a shadow world. Their names and their talents were recognized only by their peers. Some of the most brilliant photographs of the Hollywood scene have been orphaned by time, works of art by unknown artists. This is truly a shame.

Although I am well aware of the identity of many of the photographers whose work is part of this book, it was my very difficult decision to eliminate all credits from the photos, rather than to praise one artist at the expense of another whose accomplishments could not be identified.

And in so doing, I hereby dedicate this entire book to each and every one of the hundreds of photographers who provided Hollywood and the film industry with a fabulous pictorial history that will survive the erosions of time.

As proof of my sincerity in making the regrettable decision, may I add that one of the photographers victimized into anonymity by this edict is . . . myself.

MADISON S. LACY

FOREWORD

"And with that I hit him!"

These were the words of an Irishman; any Irishman is usually a little bit full of feist.

Maddy Lacy always made me think of that "Mick," and this is what got into his photos—catching the subject just as he wanted it. It took someone of Maddy's temperament to hit that moment, and that's what he did—"got" his subject at just the right moment.

There were none superior to Maddy, and this book proves it.

—JAMES CAGNEY

Hollywood Cheesecake

INTRODUCTION

If I were to count the number of people who worked with D. W. Griffith and are still around today, I wouldn't even run out of fingers.

I remember that in 1917, when the United States had just declared war on Germany but the troopships hadn't yet steamed out of New York harbor, I was in Los Angeles, a budding young law student from Philadelphia on my first visit to the not-so-woolly West, lugging the evidence of my photographic mania, a 4-by-5 Graflex camera. I had managed to meet Billy Bitzer, Griffith's cameraman, and he had given me a note approving my visit to a movie set.

By today's standards, the Triangle Griffith Studio wasn't much of a moviemaking plant. It was at the junction of Hollywood and Sunset boulevards, considerably east of what we have come to recognize as Hollywood. Just a cluster of wooden buildings including three stages. There was a shack at the entrance with benches along the walls doubling as a waiting room and a casting office. C. E. Taylor, Griffith's writer, worked in a bungalow, and the business office was on the second floor. A small, grassy square separated the stages, prop rooms, and projection rooms from the actors' dressing rooms, a long building lined with many doors leading to individual compartments. And at the end, the film laboratory, cutting rooms, and projection booths for inspecting the film.

There were no restaurant facilities. You either brought your lunch or took a noontime stroll west three blocks to Vermont Avenue and a small café.

Getting into the studio was no problem. I just walked in. No guards, no locked gates, no secretaries to bar your way. In those days the movie business was new, and visitors were more encouraged than discouraged.

The movie set I visited wasn't Griffith's *Intolerance*—and yet in a way, it was. Let me explain. *Intolerance* had cost a lot of money to film, and Griffith was trying to recoup those costs by taking sections of the original *Intolerance* and building another story. In this case it was titled *The Fall of Babylon,* and it starred Constance Talmadge, who had played the role of the mountain girl in the first film. When I met Griffith's assistant, George Seigman, I asked him if I could take some photographs. No one objected, so I hung around for two or three days, snapping

The premiere fan dancer of them all, SALLY RAND also proved to be the most enduring. In her seventies she continued to work. She died in 1979.

pictures. Naturally, I was in awe of Griffith. Everyone was. But he never demanded this. He was very personable, devoid of pretension, easily approachable but quite businesslike.

He was a taskmaster with his actors, however, addressing only his stars personally. With other performers he would tell George Seigman to tell the second assistant, Arthur Howard, to tell the players what Griffith wanted them to do. Of course, he conversed freely and often with Billy Bitzer, his cameraman. Billy was an important cog in Griffith's movie machinery. Bitzer could crank the camera and handle the panning and tilting at the same time, a skill displayed by a rare few. He also knew the correct formulas for processing the film, adding the blue dyes that turned day into night, mixing the reds and blues for other light effects, and putting the sepia tones into outdoor scenes.

I had been shooting my photographs for several days when Bitzer cornered me.

"Anybody who's crazy enough to haul around a camera that heavy ought to be paid for it," he told me.

"If that's the case, hire me," I replied.

All of a sudden I was in the movie business, hauling down the munificent sum of twelve-fifty per week, working with Woody Woodbury in the still department (my hiring had doubled the department's personnel). We would fuss around our still lab, developing and printing, making copies, and loading film holders. Then someone from the set would call us, and we'd go down and take a still picture. We'd grab a couple of glass plates and take the picture on orthochromatic film, a slow process that

They said THEDA BARA's name was an anagram for *Arab Death*, but Theodosia Goodman of Ohio knew the power of sex appeal and flaunted it during the rambunctious post–World War I era. Here she is, bedroom-eyed and beaded for her title role in the 1918 production of *Cleopatra*.

MABEL NORMAND was a comedienne, but we don't know whether this pose was for laughs. We *do* surmise she wasn't lashed up like that by Mack Sennett, who adored her. A model discovered for films by D. W. Griffith, she became the screen's greatest comedienne, only to be banned from films after two unfortunate scandals.

In 1916 this costume was daring, but ANNETTE KELLERMAN, who first gained fame with her diving-and-swimming act on the vaudeville stage, was not unused to displaying her torso. She introduced the one-piece black leotard and later appeared nude in films.

demanded at least a full second of exposure, freezing the actors and actresses in midaction poses.

Griffith operated two companies. One company starred Lillian Gish plus such performers as Henry B. Walthall, Adolph Lestina, Mae Marsh, George Fawcett, Bobby Herron, and others. The second company made films starring Dorothy Gish. Dorothy was a charming girl, a doll. So was her sister, Lillian, but Lillian was *the* star, and most of us stayed clear of her. She didn't demand that, of course, but we nevertheless accorded her that exalted status. In those days actresses didn't enjoy special privileges, but Lillian Gish did. She had the fanciest dressing room, a suite. She attended the daily rushes with Griffith, usually just the two of them viewing the film before the rest of the company saw it at a subsequent screening.

That may not sound like the privileged life of a movie star, but the status symbols that were to develop in later years were not yet in the incubators. For instance, Lillian Gish didn't have her own car and driver except on very rare occasions. She had no makeup man or special hairdresser or wardrobe mistress. She fixed her hair and face, got dressed in her costume, and reported to the set on her own. Oh, there were makeup men in those days, but they were actors who also worked to get other performers ready for the camera.

There was never concern about status when a film troupe went to some nearby location to film. There might be one limousine, though, which would transport the director general and whomever he chose to invite along. The rest of us climbed into a small bus after putting our equipment aboard a truck. Quite often we would get into our own cars and drive to the location.

The essence of life in a film studio of that era was camaraderie. Almost everyone was very young. The actresses had to be young to endure the cruelty of the early-day cameras. There was no diffusion to hide wrinkles or

CLARINE SEYMOUR, a discovery of D. W. Griffith's, was a diminutive beauty who became one of the earlier trademarked darlings of the screen when an enterprising press agent tagged her with the title Cutie Beautiful.

15

MAE MURRAY, one of the great silent stars, struck this sexy pose in a 1925 film, *Masked Bride*. One year later she became Hollywood's first princess when she married Prince David Mdivani in a well-publicized ceremony that included Pola Negri as matron of honor and Valentino as best man.

This leg-art pose of DOROTHY MACKAILL was used to publicize *Bright Lights*, a 1930 movie heralded as "a First National and Vitaphone All-Technicolor Production."

16

As she grew older, MARY PICKFORD became bolder. In *Kiki* there was no mistaking her efforts to exude sex appeal. Note those Pickford pedal extremities.

crow's-feet. It required a youthful complexion to survive the prying eye of the camera lens. It was not unusual for a member of the crew to take the film's star out on a date after work. I had dates with a dozen or so stars in those days, and so did the others. If a feminine star liked the prop man, they dated. If a camera assistant developed a crush on an actress, he asked her to go out with him.

We were one big, happy family, this motley gathering of youthful, spirited folks who gathered together to work in an industry that the world had not yet taken seriously. Like a circus or a traveling carnival, the silent-era filmmakers lived in their world within a world, turning out the varied products of an industry that specialized in manufacturing shadows. The movie colony in those days was a breed apart, and the truth is that these reckless young colonists purposely labored to keep it that way, shutting out the rest of the world while they went cheerfully about a business that all others were unable to fathom.

We had our own world—and were damned proud of it.

ANN PENNINGTON went from the stage and Flo Ziegfeld dancing roles to movie musicals. It's easy to see why she was enormously successful from coast to coast.

17

A publicist by the name of Lincoln Quarberg christened JEAN HARLOW the Platinum Blonde, a tag that stayed with her throughout her flamboyant life as a movie star.

About that time I took my first movie-leg-art photograph. I snapped a picture of Lillian Gish with her feet up on a chair, exposing her leg clear up to midcalf. Go ahead and laugh, if you wish, but in those days, my friend, that was a sexy photo. It was even risqué.

But it was to be many years before my love affair with leg art blossomed into a total romance.

Anyway, there I was in this crazy, mixed-up movie business and the living was easy. Together with two other crew members, I rented a big house on Vermont Avenue, just a few blocks north of Hollywood Boulevard. It cost sixty dollars a month, and we lived very well indeed. In those days the action was not in Hollywood or Beverly Hills or Malibu. It was downtown. The number-one hotel was the Alexandria, and it remained so until the Ambassador Hotel arose on Wilshire Boulevard. The stars, who were young and attractive and were getting more money than they'd ever seen in their lives, looked for entertainment in areas like Watts and Central Avenue, the old Vernon Country Club, the Sunset Inn above Santa Monica, the Tumble Inn between Venice and Ocean Park, or the Ship Café on the Venice pier.

We worked a six-day week but rarely at night. However, I remember one film that was shot at night, *Battling Jane,* starring Dorothy Gish, Carole Dempster, and Richard Barthelmess. The set was a Sixth Street chocolate shop, and we could film only after their daily close of business.

A rare pose in which VERONICA LAKE exposes both her eyes to the camera. Her habit of covering one eye with her hair earned her the title the Peekaboo Girl. Often starred opposite Alan Ladd, Veronica died in 1973 at 53.

19

A great glamour star, RITA HAYWORTH (originally named Rita Cansino) started in films as a stock girl at 20th Century-Fox. She was the wife of Orson Welles and Aly Khan.

In those days film was highly perishable, and the negative couldn't be moved about much without suffering. So they'd line up a second camera and ship its negative abroad for printing foreign versions of the movie. Occasionally, I got to crank that second camera. It was fun, but it didn't put any more dollars into the paycheck.

New Horizons

After a year and a half in the employ of D. W. Griffith, that itch known as impetuous youth got me scratching toward other goals. I moved on to Hal Roach studios and became a jack of all trades. I'd put on makeup and play an extra or do a bit role. I'd assist anyone who needed assistance. We were doing the Lonesome Luke comedies starring Harold Lloyd, and I had a guarantee of fifteen dollars a week. We'd shoot a comedy in three days. One-reelers. If I worked four days, I was paid twenty dollars, with an added five dollars for a fifth day. At the end of each comedy, a photographer would be hired from a downtown studio. He'd come out to the set for a half day and shoot the stills.

One day I said to Roach's assistant, Freddie Newmeyer, that I'd like to shoot the stills, and Freddie suggested I talk it over with Roach. I barged in on him—he was head of his own studio, but he didn't have a secretary—and told him: "Look, I'm a photographer, and I could do other things too."

Roach inquired about my equipment, and I told him I had my own 8-by-10 view camera.

"Go order a dozen plates and show me what you can do," he suggested.

So I ordered two dozen plates, shot each of the dozen poses with different exposure settings, and selected the best ones to show Hal Roach.

"I'll start you at twenty-five dollars a week," he decided. That meant *every* week. I was in seventh heaven.

An early pose of LANA TURNER, the beauty who earned lasting fame as the Sweater Girl.

DOROTHY LAMOUR didn't always require a sarong to display her delightful figure.

An early leg-art pose of ANN SHERIDAN, pre–Warner Bros., when she was first under contract as a starlet at Paramount as a result of winning a beauty contest.

MARION DAVIES rows merrily along and proves that T-shirt grafitti are not a seventies discovery.

Hollywood beckoned JOAN BLONDELL, along with James Cagney, from the Broadway stage in 1930. Forty-eight years later, she was still performing in starring parts, latest with Jon Voight and Faye Dunaway in MGM's *The Champ*.

For the next four years I was Harold Lloyd's still photographer. And I was also an assistant director. And I ran the studio still laboratory, developing, printing, and distributing. And I ran errands. And I drove cars to locations. And I was a unit manager, a business manager, an associate producer, occasionally a second-unit director, and anything else that was being done by someone who happened to be home sick. And finally I had a talented assistant, Gene Kornman, and I was drawing forty-five dollars a week. We were covering all the Roach comedies, the Harold Lloyds, the Our Gangs, and the Snub Pollards.

And then Hal Roach started making comedies starring Eddie "Bo" Boland, recruiting a half dozen pretty girls to perform with Boland in the Vanity Fair Maids comedies.

That was the official beginning of the Lacy–Leg-art Love Affair. Oh, sure, I'd immortalized an occasional exposed female limb in other one-reelers, but the Vanity Fair Maids were leg art personified. More than 150 pretty girls showed up for the auditions—and more about that later on—and six were finally selected. For a solid year we made one comedy a week with the Vanity Fair Maids and Eddie "Bo" Boland. The action was designed for both laughs and leg art. The girls did crazy things—jumping up on a couch when a mouse strolled in, caught out in the forest with a cannibal king, cavorting as harem girls with Boland as the sheik, anything to blend the figures with the fun.

Later, I plunked down $3,715 for a Bell and Howell movie camera and photographed a Ruth Roland serial directed by George Marshall. I had quit the Roach studios after a hassle with Hal Roach's father, who was treasurer of the company. He thought I spent too much money while I was assistant director on a film made at a nearby beach. For almost a year I bummed around the West Coast until I was flat broke.

Then I returned to the movies as an extra and occasional stunt double. Finally, a friend and I formed the Foreign Auto Car Rental Agency, buying cars and renting them to the movies and occasionally doing car stunts for films. Along the line I acquired a casting office, and for three years I fooled everyone into thinking I was an expert casting director. By 1928 I was a long distance away from my beloved leg art.

On August 1, 1928, the cameramen formed a union and sought out members to build a show of strength. At first I resisted, but they talked me into joining.

"What'll it cost me?" I asked. They said an initiation fee for a first cameraman would be $25.00; second cameramen would pay $17.50; and a still photographer could get in for

RUBY KEELER, a dancing star with Ziegfeld, emerged as a major screen personality opposite Dick Powell in *42nd Street* and married Al Jolson.

CAROLE LANDIS—Stardom came to her in *One Million B.C.* opposite Victor Mature and ended with her mysterious and untimely death in 1948 at the age of 29.

Before MARIE MC DONALD came into films and earned a worldwide recognition as the Body, she had been a band singer with Tommy Dorsey. Her life was never really happy, and her untimely death was tragic.

A budding actress in 1948, MARILYN MONROE had a small
part in the Marx Brothers' *Love Happy*. Groucho saw
her, liked her looks, and called in photographer
Madison Lacy to take this and other pictures of her.

$10.00. Naturally, being a bit short in the wallet, I ordered the $10.00 special. After all, I was still in the car and casting business.

Oh, how I would love to have those cars today! We had fifty-six of them—Pierce-Arrows, Stutzes, Hispano-Suizas, and Mercedeses, Rolls-Royces, Duesenbergs, Fiats, Packards, Chandlers, an Auburn. When I decided to have my personal Sunbeam painted, I took it to Earl C. Anthony. It cost me $533, but that included the nickeling. After all, a $17,400 automobile specially built by Anthony in Pasadena from a chassis I picked up in New York deserved the very best makeup. And while it was being painted I dug out $600 for a Stutz Bulldog to keep me on the streets in the interim.

After I sold my casting office and grew tired of loafing, I got a job shooting stills for Willis Kent, who was producing States Rights pictures. His films were made without any distribution partnership. He'd finish a movie, then go out and sell the film in individual states. That meant a bit of a wait for crew members like myself while he unloaded his last effort and began filming his next one.

So I went to Trem Carr. His headquarters was in the heart of Gower Gulch, an area at Sunset Boulevard and Gower where the cowboys hung out, waiting for calls to work in westerns. Trem Carr made westerns—lots of them. About *every* fifteenth movie or so, he'd make a *big* western. Shucks, pardner, they'd shoot those "outdoor epics" as long as three weeks. My life was delightful, if dusty.

Then one day a stranger rode into town and headed me off at the pass. Actually, it was Trem Carr's brother, who worked as a cameraman for another company. One day Trem called me in and told me, "My brother lost his job, and now I'm either going to have to hire him or support him. I can't add an extra cameraman, and my brother likes to take still pictures. What do you say to all that?"

I had the perfect answer to that one. "Goodbye, Trem," I replied.

Here is France's Sex Kitten BRIGITTE BARDOT at age twenty, as she prepared for her first English-speaking star role in the British comedy *Doctor at Sea*. Parisians called her La Belle Bardot.

27

CHILI WILLIAMS made few films but became famous worldwide as the Polkadot Girl, modeling spotted fashions for a clothing manufacturer.

But I didn't hang my head and ride off into the sunset. A brand-new type of motion picture had been born along with the birth of sound on the screen. The musical. Music to the ears of a leg-art lothario. Beautiful girls in scanty costumes. Trim ankles, shapely calves, luscious thighs.

Legs. Legs! *Legs!*

Fifteen years after I had walked in on a D. W. Griffith set, bulky camera in hand, and had pointed its lens at the mountain girl, Constance Talmadge, my life in the movies was really just beginning—the part of that life I enjoyed most: the leg-art days.

Of the stars whom D. W. Griffith recruited for his earliest movies, only two boasted any stage experience. One of them was BLANCHE SWEET, shown here in a much later leg-art pose. The other was a sixteen-year-old named Mary Pickford.

28

Showing off her legs in this publicity pose, AGNES AYRES demonstrates why Valentino couldn't resist sweeping her into his arms and carrying her off to a tryst in *The Sheik*. Seventeen years after that film, Agnes was on tour, lured from obscurity to vaudeville to promote the rerelease of *The Sheik*, brought back in 1938 as a talkie that didn't talk but offered some stirring background music.

When it came to pretty legs, CAROLE LOMBARD had them. She also had talent—as demonstrated engagingly with William Powell in *My Man Godfrey* and with Fredric March in *Nothing Sacred*.

The world's number-one pinup queen, BETTY GRABLE, died in 1973 at fifty-six.

MARIE PREVOST was one of Mack Sennett's prettiest and most popular bathing beauties, but sound movies ended her reign as a romantic comedienne, reducing her to supporting roles calling for little or no dialogue. Crushed by her demotion, Marie took to drink.

LEG ART

Its early days from Mythology to Mazepa

It's not a very attractive term, *leg art*. Very little glamour, appeal, or pizazz. Certainly it offers very little competition to its many fancier-named cousins—*cheesecake, pinup, centerfold*.

But what leg art lacks in ear appeal it more than makes up in *eye* appeal. And through the years its effect on the photography of the feminine form has been historic. It represents great milestones in the heralded chronological events that led women from the hesitant exposure of an ankle to today's brash and uninhibited displays of rose-tinted human flesh from cowlick to carbuncle, all in full color, dead straight into the camera lens, no privates too private, innuendoes shouted aloud instead of insinuated.

One would have to drift back to the era of mythology to find the original progenitors of leg art as we recognize it today. All through the classic accounts of life among the gods of antiquity, the feminine form proved a dominant factor. Early history often spotlights the many young and beautiful females who were chosen to participate in religious rites. Some of these beauties were dancers, moving sinuously to the tempos of chants, drumbeats, handclaps, or incantations. Invariably the chosen maiden was sparsely clad or, in many instances, completely nude. As she moved gracefully through the ceremonial rituals, there was rarely any doubt that her sex and her beauty were important elements of the program. But her legs weren't.

Even the great artists, the painters whose delineations of women *au naturel* have survived the centuries to be accorded greater adoration with each passing decade, chose to accent more vividly the face, the neck, the bosom, the navel, and the hip, leaving the legs to stand, dangle, or curl in utter anonymity—depending on the postures of action or repose. Titian's exquisite flesh tones were mostly of the cheek, chest, and flank, rarely of the kneecap, ankle, or calf. Oh, sure, many of the great artists shaped the feminine limb masterfully. Michelangelo, with his superb understanding of the human anatomy, shaped a leg as perfectly as any other portion of the human figure. But it would take an art student much more observant than I to pinpoint a Michelangelo masterpiece that paid undivided homage to the female leg.

Not until society's manners and morals chose

33

to hide the feminine leg from casual view did it begin to develop as a total sex symbol. The Victorian gentleman—using the term advisedly—went ape at the briefest sight of an exposed ankle. In the show-everything era of the eighties, an exposed ankle rates about .0001 on a scale of ten, but in the nineteenth century it was double dynamite.

The female leg had finally made its mark. The low degree of public display had heightened its sensuality. Men began to pay money just to look at girls' legs. In Montmartre, Paris, where Lautrec and his fellow artists had captured on canvas the sexual aura of a neighborhood considered at that time to be the naughtiest in the universe, the celebrated Can-Can girls came to life. Their high kicks, which showed their stockings, garters, and lace panties, endeared them to the predominantly male audiences; and when, with their ear-piercing squeals, they went into their full splits, one by one, many of their admirers were already standing on top of their chairs, roaring huzzahs.

America couldn't stand the vast distance between Manhattan and Montmartre. Soon the Can-Can girls were also in the United States, imported by entrepreneurs who knew the best ways to corral the entertainment dollar. But the rustle of many skirts, the yips and splits, the Gallic leg show could not captivate forever. Other areas of entertainment had to be explored.

Enter Ada Isaacs Mencken as the immortal Mazepa, strapped astride a stallion, crossing a theater stage clad in skin-colored leotards as she immortalized the historic equestrian peregrination of Lady Godiva. Ada Isaacs Mencken made history in more ways than one. She also became the first actress to be identified by a descriptive phrase. She was the Naked Lady.

And now tights had become *de rigueur* as female entertainers of the stage placed the big accent on the anatomical curve. The awesome bustline competed with the ample hipline, separated by the most infinitesimal of waistlines. America had discovered another phenomenon—the hourglass figure.

The full-figured femme had become something of a symbol along the frontiers of America too. In various stages of nudity, she went along with the trailblazer, the Indian fighter, and the pioneer to help open and establish the western frontiers of America. The classic saloon of the early West became her home away from home. The dancehall girl of the West ranked alongside such frontier immortals as Buffalo Bill and Kit Carson and Jim Bowie. She moved with the desperadoes, too. For every Billy the Kid there was a Calamity Jane. For every James brother there was a Moustache Mary.

But even better than being in the bar was being on display *over* the bar. The celebrated paintings of reclining nudes gazing languidly at the cowboy tossing off his shotglass of redeye can still be found prominently displayed in the watering holes of western towns that still use the legends of the early west to attract the tourist trade. What the Betty Grable pinup was to the GI of World War II, the unclad ladies over the saloon bar were to the frontiersman, who probably knew what he was fighting Redskins and rustlers for. It sure's hell wasn't for mom and apple pie.

Paintings in those days kept the virile man hopeful. Except for an occasional daguerreotype, photography had not yet begun to immortalize the feminine form divine. There were perhaps three paintings that got the job done better than others.

September Morn showed the greatest potential for immortality. The young woman, shorn of clothing, stood ankle deep in the water of the lake, shivering against the chill. Her hands concealed her pubic region, and a self-embracing arm hid her breasts. A childlike creature, she epitomized every virtue of innocent erotica. Her appeal was so universal that she moved from canvas to calendar—in fact, eight million calendars!

34

This photo of MARY PICKFORD, America's Sweetheart, showed less leg than some but gave her a mature look, and for that reason Little Mary actually looked sexy.

When it came to posing for leg art, the D. W. Griffith star LILLIAN GISH was considerably less than enthusiastic, but occasionally the action demanded in a movie scene would put the Gish gams on display. Here she is, and there they are, in a scene from the 1918 film *The Greatest Thing in Life*, Adolphe Lestina portrayed her father.

In contrast to her superstar sister, Lillian, DOROTHY GISH was much less shy about leg art. In this scene from *Nell Gwynn*, she demonstrates the plight of the garterless girl.

September Morn was an early and glowing example of provocative press agentry. The artist, Paul Chabas, recognizing that notoriety was what gave the artist the most lucrative commissions (often more so than talent), hired a publicist to glorify his skills. The press agent talked a New York shopkeeper into displaying *September Morn* in his store window. Next, he hired a group of children to stand in front of the window and gape at the revealing artwork. Last, he put in a call to the New York Society for the Prevention of Vice and expressed the vehement protestations of a scandalized citizen. When the society answered his outraged appeal, the innocent maiden standing in the lake began her swift journey from an insignificant store window to newspaper headlines and international fame.

Notoriety was what usually led the gorgeous unclad beauties from canvas to global acclaim. *The Naked Maja,* which later became the subject of a well-received motion picture starring Ava Gardner, was another work of art that scandalized a nation. Yet on the wave of its storm of condemnations, *The Naked Maja* eventually became famous, then accepted,

Seminudity was a fact of life for BETTY BLYTHE, even in the silent era. In *Queen of Sheba*, filmed at the height of the Flapper era, Betty became a symbol of the liberated woman of that period just as Rudolph Valentino was the ideal encouraging men to become sheiks in the Roaring Twenties.

It was a good idea and a pretty publicity pose, but DOROTHY DALTON'S idea of white shoe and stocking for one leg and black for the other didn't catch on.

A rare early bathing-beauty publicity photo, considered to be quite daring, especially for a star of Priscilla Deane's magnitude. Perhaps the flag around her waist made the pose more patriotic and less exotic.

finally adored, and ultimately an official Spanish postage stamp.

Then there was the glorious Stella. Whether or not she had drawn her origin from the fame of *The Naked Maja,* Stella was a truly qualified rival. She was strictly show business. Painted on canvas in life-sized dimensions, the delightfully nude beauty was a traveling attraction for almost two decades during the twenties and thirties. Her "booking agents" would come into a town, rent a small vacant shop in a downtown area, and put Stella on display. Hung in a dark recess of the store or framed in a shadowbox, the frontal view of her reclining nudity drew anxious customers who paid anywhere from ten to twenty-five cents, depending on the state of the local economy, to stare at her magnificent charms. On many occasions Stella seemed to offer a three-dimensional appearance, and many a believing patron stood patiently for a long, long time waiting for her to blink just once.

While many a man hung *September Morn* in his home, adored the undraped *Maja,* and waited for Stella to wink just once, photography was beginning to take up where the artist's brush strokes had stopped. In the penny arcades the cherished Kinetoscope had arrived front and center. One dropped a coin in the slot, put one's eyes to the binocular viewing apparatus, began turning the crank as the light bulb came on inside the machine, and presto! A full wheel of individual photos began flopping one over the other, giving full and complete motion to the subject. The subject, of course, was invariably feminine, and her actions consisted in either taking off her clothes, dancing seductively in a skimpy costume, showering kisses on a receptive male partner, or performing whatever act could be devised to suggest sexual activity without showing it.

And with the Kinetoscope, of course, came the self-appointed censors. Reform groups began to question the moral integrity of the Kinetoscope. That little crank on the side of the ornately decorated contrivance could fall into the unwitting grasp of an innocent child, they screamed.

Of course, they were right.

I was one of those innocent children. Without any knowledge of what might suddenly appear before my eyes, I had walked many blocks from home to the penny arcade, had stealthily worked my way toward the Kinetoscope, and had patiently awaited my opportunity. No one around? No one looking? Whoosh! The coin was in the slot, my pudgy little baby fist was gripping the crank, my baby-blue eyes approached the viewing glass, and the photographs were dropping into place as fast as my childish attempt at cranking could make them fall. The saints forbid that some adult should leap forward and halt my cranking before the show was completed!

The reform groups were absolutely right. Disregarding the fragile texture of my infantile psyche, that pretty lady inside the box was surely performing her lascivious gyrations. It was a terrible experience to be suffered by a mere child. And what made it even worse, the Kinetoscope viewer was five feet above the floor, and I was only four feet two. What a nasty trick to play on a little kid!

Her hula is perhaps as authentic as that palmy painted backdrop, but there was nothing phony about the sex appeal of BETTY COMPSON, a leading lady to the deformed cripple in the 1920 movie *The Miracle Man*, which sent Lon Chaney on his way to immortal fame as *The Man of a Thousand Faces*.

In *The Woman Who Fooled Herself* MAY ALLISON, togged in the tools of her trade as a show-biz siren, gets roses from a hidden admirer.

THE DAY
THAT LEG MET ART

Leg art came into existence as if by Caesarean section. It required a lot of outside assistance to achieve life. Perhaps that was because the phrase, as we mentioned before, is not a particularly palatable expression. There could have been dozens of exotic, alluring, provocative tags to identify photographs of pretty girls of the movies, but on the day leg art first drew breath as a coined expression, the movie business was still strutting around like a cocky young kid, forsaking the gentilities of the spoken word as it pared off great slices of glamour and skimmed them toward a waiting world like Frisbees.

Pete Smith, the energetic, worldly-wise director of publicity for Metro-Goldwyn-Mayer, is the man who launched the tag *leg art*. Later, he was to go on to become producer of a long series of those highly entertaining screen short subjects that bore his name, but in his flacking days he was a powerful force behind the great ascendancies to stardom of many of Metro-Goldwyn-Mayer's vast stable of starlets and hopefuls. In those days around the lair of Leo the Lion, anything photographic was known as *art*. There were portrait art, costume art, cinema art, publicity art—the list goes on and on. Whenever MGM sent out a publicist and a photographer to immortalize a starlet or star, Pete's final instruction was inevitably the same: "Get some good leg art!"

Gradually the phrase crept into the lexicon of the movie business, where trick words and phrases were being invented daily to describe the artifacts and the activities of putting images on the screen. A cute dish would hike up her tight skirt, perch on her luggage at the railway station, and pose for a Hollywood arrival shot, and the next day a panting publicity planter would burst into a newspaper city room and shout, "Boy, have I got leg art for you today!"

She wasn't Susie Smith, runner-up to Miss America. She wasn't the studio's answer to Clara Bow. She wasn't the most promising young actress west of the Alleghenies. She wasn't the dazzled unknown about to begin her film career at the top. She was leg art.

It is a fitting tribute to the belief that plain talk is invincible that the phrase *leg art* has prospered and survived for more than fifty years. Hollywood is enjoying its fourth generation of leg art. Even the progenitor of leg art is alive and kicking.

Leg art's parent, as any lens louse will tell

BILLIE DOVE was a dazzling beauty with a figure to match. Most of her film roles were sexy, and some of her later films helped stimulate a cry for film censorship. But until the Hays Office clamped down on cinema sex, Billie Dove was man's favorite bird.

Pretty legs have always been utilized to great promotional advantage in selling the public a new fad. HELENE CHADWICK does her best to keep a straight face while her gams are used to promote the popular game of mah jong.

you, was cheesecake. The use of *cheesecake* in this context has a very suspect ancestry. It depends on which unimpeachable old-timer you talk to. Two of the three most popular versions concern photographic coverage of shipboard arrivals. In the first version, a well-known entertainment star arrived on a ship from Europe and was asked by a news photographer to sit on the ship's railing in order to display a bit more of her lovely ankles, calves, and knees. The lady willingly obliged, and when the photographer popped the photo in front of the eyes of his editor, the gentleman pushed back his green visor and, inasmuch as he prided himself as a gourmet, pronounced with considerable authority that the pose was tastier than cheesecake.

I don't like that version either.

Version number two is quite similar, but this particular photographer carried his lunch box with him as he covered the daily ship arrivals, and it invariably included a slice of his wife's cheesecake. The pretty ship passenger—some insist she was a famous opera star—obliged his request for a leg show, whereupon the ogling cameraman exclaimed, "Boy, that's as good as my wife's cheesecake!"

How the rest of the world managed to eavesdrop on this statement aboard a liner in the eyeline of the Statue of Liberty and send the word *cheesecake* winging on its way to global acceptance is a chain of events I cannot—you should excuse the expression—swallow.

The third version is landlocked. It concerns a portrait photographer who invariably referred to his subject's bosom as cupcakes. He also utilized the familiar request that his subject say, "Cheese," to elicit the proper smile. Between the bosom and the smile he decided an amalgamation of the two words would best describe what he was after.

Personally, I think all three stories are equally true and false. I can't deny that they may have happened; I don't believe that any one of them (or all three, for that matter) sponsored the

NORMA TALMADGE enjoyed twenty years of stardom, but the advent of sound drowned out her career. When critics blasted Norma's second talkie, sister Connie wired her: "Leave them while you're looking good and thank God for the trust funds Mama set up."

One of the few stage stars who responded to the lure of the movies, ALLA NAZIMOVA used her sexy lines and lack of inhibition to emerge quickly as a popular screen siren. At one time her costume designer was Natacha Rambova, later to marry Rudolph Valentino.

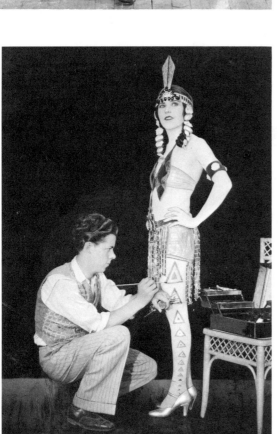

No one could object to an exposed leg as long as there was a reason for showing it. Here's a very youthful Perc Westmore, of the heralded Westmore makeup clan, putting the Indian sign on RUTH ROLAND to publicize a 1924 movie, *The Masked Woman*.

word. Expressions have a way of evolving from a widely separated series of situations, events, and inspirations that somehow travel divergent paths toward popularity. Somewhere along the line they meet and lend their combined weights and strengths to create the sonic boom that places the word or expression in a state of public acceptance.

With your indulgence, I would like to introduce you to a fourth version of how the photographic cheesecake was baked. A veritable horde of photographers, most of whom used the "Say 'Cheese'" order to provoke a smile, pointed their cameras at very pretty girls at the same time and without each other's knowledge. Each in his own way sought the "extra inch" that would make the photo more delightful. To take a pretty picture of a pretty girl in a pretty pose that displays her pretty charms does wonderful things to one's tastebuds. Even the tastebuds of photographers. The minute someone—one of the three shutterbugs who claim the honor, perhaps—called it cheesecake, that same horde of photographers rolled their eyes, licked their lips, and agreed.

Tasty, man, tasty!

A swimsuit designer might manufacture two dozen of today's beach styles from the water togs worn by GLORIA SWANSON as a Mack Sennett Bathing Beauty.

CLAIRE WINDSOR, a reigning beauty of the silent screen, rarely posed for leg art, but it was a nice, summery day on location in Greenwich, Connecticut, for *Born Rich*, the sun was at her back, the gardens were lovely, the gown was gossamer—so why not?

45

A dramatic actress who rarely exposed a leg for the camera, CORINNE GRIFFITH was another silent-day star who succumbed to the pitfalls of sound movies. Unlike many others, however, she endured her cinematic downfall to write several books, invest in Southern California real estate, dabble in politics, and emerge as one of the wealthiest ex-stars of them all.

THE BIG SHOW IN SHOW BIZ

Legs never left show business after the first high kick under a spotlight aimed at center stage. Sally Rand, with her magnificent fans and bubbles that teased audiences into roaring ovations, was a headline act for many decades. Even as this was written, Sally Rand was still around, making patterns with her feathers just as she did back at the World's Fair in Chicago more than forty years ago.

But in Sally's heyday the stripteasers were taking over the show-business limelight, all the way from the sleaziest saloon to the brightest, brassiest, and most expensive watering holes of the world. Girls with gorgeous bodies were getting rich by undressing in public. Some were perhaps clumsy, albeit curvaceous. Others were true artists, deserving of the title. Their acts were carefully honed, the lighting effects were dramatic, and the music breathed sensuality. As the competition among stripping stars grew, the novelty approaches to strippers became more and more bizarre. One stripper shed her garments with the help of a flock of trained doves. Another allowed her charms to be exposed in flashes from behind the coils of snakes encircling her body. Women with tassels

attached to their breasts did wondrous things with them. The bodies were invariably beautiful, but it was the techniques used in displaying them that spelled the difference between a headline booking in a metropolitan nightclub and a two-week stint on a makeshift stage behind a neighborhood bar.

In Paris the Folies-Bergère were dominating the tourist dollar, and on Broadway Florenz Ziegfeld was packing them in. George White and Earl Carroll were working overtime to cut into the fortunes raked in by the man they called Flo. In later years New York's most famous theater of the day, the celebrated Roxy, was to cover its giant stage from wing to wing with gorgeous legs moving and kicking in perfect unison as the world-renowned Rockettes precision kicked their way to everlasting prominence in show biz.

In politics the candidate with the greatest number of supporters who were feminine, were attractive, and had shapely legs well on display inevitably drew the big crowds. In restaurants the waitresses with short skirts that became even shorter when they leaned over to serve a bug-eyed male customer were helping to keep

MAE MARSH, one of D. W. Griffith's most winsome stars, is shown here in her role for *Polly of the Circus*. She was also one of the stars of one of the greatest films of the time, Griffith's *The Birth of a Nation*.

MARY MILES MINTER was at the apex of her career when she became a victim of the mysterious death of William Desmond Taylor. Indiscreet love letters she wrote to the director were published, shattering her pure screen image. This leg-art pose by Minter illustrated stories of her involvement in the unsolved mystery.

business booming. On the fields of sport the strong, husky male athletes were sharing the entertaining of the spectators with the glistening drum majorettes in scanty costumes or the leaping cheerleaders in tight sweaters and skimpy skirts.

Beauty contests were exploding everywhere. Judges gave critical attention to the pretty girl's profile, her talent in everything from song to sewing, and her poise as a public speaker. Then they chose the girl who did more for a bathing suit than any of the others. Good legs still conquered brains.

The female figure was heavily exploited in the world of advertising, too. Of course, that had been going on since the 1850s. Great Grandpa's eye strayed more than once—and remained there longer than required—to a nineteenth-century corset advertisement, not to mention such other unmentionables as garters, hosiery, and high-button shoes. Even in those days, any excuse to show a bit more of the feminine form than was normal proved an eye-catcher.

Pretty girls and commercial products have gone hand in hand for more than a century, and the romance is still on. One wonders what shape advertising would have taken if leg art had been outlawed by an act of Congress. Just the thought is enough to make a grown man cry.

And yet it is ironic that when the movies moved from the Kinetoscope to an image on a screen that could be enjoyed by more than one person at a time, leg art was a rarity. Oh, one might view a fleeting scene or two of a girl dancer in a tutu, but the showing of the female figure was a rare sight until the teens of the twentieth century. Then, little by little, public demand began to make itself heard. And so did the motion-picture publicist. He began to tell the public that those interesting shadows on the screen were actually people. They had names, they were artistic, and one of them could possibly be more alluring than another. The costumes became more elaborate, and photographs were made of the performers in costume. The photos were used to advertise the photoplay and the artist. This metamorphosis took place over several years, but eventually screen actors began to achieve personal identification. The public was demanding to know who they were and what they were. The moviemakers were coerced into putting the names of the players up on the screen.

Newspapers and magazines were also well aware of the virtues of a pretty girl with a pretty figure. Pictures of movie actresses in slightly abbreviated costumes began to pop up on the printed page. Many a legitimate news item bit the dust as a girlie photo took the space away.

About this time Mack Sennett was dominating the comedy-film scene with his crazy Keystone Kops. The Kops and Mabel Normand were fast becoming the biggest attractions on the screen. But as funny as they were in action, the Keystone Kops couldn't get their pictures in the papers. Who would ever prefer a portrait of cross-eyed Ben Turpin to a bathing-suit picture of a charming lady?

Sennett was a showman. If it took girls to get his films publicized in the press, let there be girls. As he recalled later in his book *King of Comedy,* Sennett had picked up a Los Angeles newspaper back in 1914, and there on page one was a three-column photograph of a pretty girl in a leggy pose. She had been involved in some minor traffic accident. Not until he got to page four did Sennett read about a speech by President Woodrow Wilson on the war crisis. The handwriting was on the wall. His comedy stars could get into the papers—linked with pretty girls showing dimpled knees. Sennett hired the prettiest girls he could find, put them in beach attire, and made sure their arms were closely linked with his Keystone Kops so newspaper editors couldn't easily crop out the comics and show only the girls.

By today's standards those bathing suits were ludicrous. There was more material in their swimsuits than is required today for ski togs.

The necklines were high, the legs of the swimsuits reached to just above the knee, and overskirts furnished additional concealment. The girls usually wore slippers and half-hose that left only the kneecaps exposed. As if that weren't enough, the girls often added floppy-brimmed hats and umbrellas.

Just before America entered World War I, Sennett did another great favor for the redblooded American male. He introduced (and, for all I know, may have originated) the beauty contest. It was held at one of his favorite movie sites, the beach at Venice, California. Girls who considered their figures extra-special were invited to join the contest and prove it. The girls showed up in droves. So did the crowds and the reporters and the cameras. Just how legitimate the contest was will never be authenticated; by some strange quirk of fate, Mack Sennett's bathing beauties finished first, second, and third!

It didn't take long for the Sennett Bathing

Beauties to begin making waves in the movie business. Other moviemakers turned to adding pretty girls to their comedy casts as well as using them photographically to exploit the films. Along came the Fox Sunshine Girls. Along came the Hal Roach Vanity Fair Maids. Even the makers of more dramatic film fare began to capitalize on leg shows. An actress whose husband had left her with two hungry kids stopped her sniffling long enough to adjust a garter or straighten a hosiery seam. An innocent maiden, unaware that the man to whom she was talking was a lascivious wastrel (that's what we used to call 'em, son), cheerfully unfastened a few buttons on her blouse to see better how pretty the new necklace looked. The country bumpkin, trying to locate his missing cousin backstage, unwittingly blundered into the chorus girls' dressing room. Not too subliminal, perhaps, but quite effective.

Three unidentified Mack Sennett bathing beauties romp on the Pacific sands close to Castle Rock, a spot immortalized in many early silent films.

This seminude pose by BESSIE LOVE undoubtedly predated her many roles as the innocent damsel in William S. Hart westerns.

As *Peter Pan*, diminutive VIOLA DANA strikes a commanding and leafy pose.

The relationship between a bouquet and a buggy whip is tenuous, but the legs certainly do match well on SHIRLEY MASON, Viola Dana's pretty sister and a star in the early years of Hollywood.

51

The VANITY FAIR MAIDS shared honors with Eddie "Bo" Boland in a series of 1920 Hal Roach two-reel comedies.

THE VANITY FAIR MAIDS

It was around 1920 or 1921, as I recall, that Hal Roach decided that Mack Sennett was nobody's fool. Roach was making a comedy a week starring Eddie "Bo" Boland, and he decided a bevy of cuties couldn't hurt the pictures. He planned to select six different girls who would become known as the Vanity Fair Maids. Each would be treated as an individual instead of just another pretty face in a line of pretty faces. Roach was seeking different types—a tiny blonde, a tall brunette, a medium-sized redhead, and so on. The girls would all wear different costumes, to avoid any uniform look. In one comedy a Vanity Fair Maid might be gowned in a floor-length formal, the next week in a peekaboo dance costume, the following week in a bathing suit. Sometimes only one or two of the girls could be viewed in leggy outfits. But never, never fewer than one.

My job was to test the aspirants during the search for the Vanity Fair Maids, and more than one hundred hopefuls showed up for the auditions. I was to make my tests via still photographs instead of movie film—an economy measure—so an exterior area was enclosed by a series of false walls called flats, which were no more than canvas stretched tightly over frames, then braced to stand upright. The girls were to wear bathing suits or whatever they felt would best show off their figures. No outright nudity, mind you, but some of them tended to want to show a bit more than the others.

Anyway, I went merrily about my work. By the second day I began to notice something strange. The canvas on the flats didn't seem to be holding up very well. Small holes began appearing in it everywhere. Further, where the holes were somewhat larger than the others, an occasional rolling eyeball could be glimpsed. I said nothing about this, however, and just went about my chores of photographing the girls. Obviously, workmen on the Hal Roach studio lot were deeply grateful that I ignored their peepholes and allowed them to rubberneck. For many weeks thereafter I was always introduced by studio workers to newcomers as "that lucky still photog."

The half dozen survivors of that delightful photo session became the Vanity Fair Maids, and they continued to perform just as often for the still camera as for the movie lens.

One of the Vanity Fair Maids at the Hal Roach studios was the beautiful Ethel Broadhurst, who had come from the East to seek her fortune in films. I believe she had been a dancer in New York, but she never told me that. One day I was lining up the Vanity Fair Maids on a staircase banister for a group shot that also included the comedy star Eddie "Bo" Boland. I was just about to take the picture, when I noticed that Broadhurst was considerably less than happy. In fact, tears were running down her cheeks. Tears just don't fit well in comedies, so I gave everyone a short break and took Ethel aside. What was her trouble? I asked. A broken romance? Illness in the family? An unpaid debt? No, Ethel's great problem concerned status. Posing along a banister with five other girls made her feel like a chorus girl—and she never again wanted to feel like that. It took a lot of talking about people who have to start somewhere in order to better themselves, newcomers who have to take their knocks early if they want to become stars later, the old path-to-stardom-is-seldom-smooth bromide. Finally, Broadhurst dried her tears, forced a smile, and went up on the banister to take another step toward stardom.

A choice morsel of early leg art, Ethel Broadhurst was one of the Vanity Fair Maidens who appeared in comedies with Eddie "Bo" Boland. She was a Broadway chorine who came West for film stardom and ended up as a Hollywood chorine.

JEAN HARLOW made her screen debut via walk-on roles in Hal Roach two-reel comedies. In view of her great fame, it is difficult to realize that when she died during the filming of *Saratoga*, she was only twenty-six years old.

THE NAME IS
THE FAME OF THE GAME
From the Naked Lady and the Biograph Girl
to Oomph and Ping

It is with a great deal of sadness that I must confess the movies seem to have discarded the lovely old custom of identifying an actress by a trademark name. Maybe we've become too sophisticated for such things. Perhaps it is because press agentry has moved out of the bawdyhouse and into the penthouse, discarding slapstick for sophistication. The one thing that seems to have gone out of publicity is fun. Too many publicists today insist that they are communications counselors or marketing specialists. No one wants to be known simply as a press agent.

And no one seems inclined to promote another Sweater Girl, Oomph Girl, or Ping Girl.

Very sad indeed.

Fortunately, we still have our trademarked beauties of the past. And their names will live forever, long after most of the current crop of movie lovelies have faded from the screen and their names have dropped from the marquees into the sea of forgetfulness.

The Naked Lady

As mentioned earlier, the first actress to be identified by a trademark was Ada Isaacs

Mencken, whose stage performances as Lady Godiva had earned her the nickname the Naked Lady. However, when Mencken would make her immortal trip across a stage strapped astride a stallion, the nudity was more implied than actual. Fact is, she really wore skin-toned leotards in her dramatic canter as the Saxon lady who demonstrated against burdensome taxes along the streets of Coventry.

The Biograph Girl

Ironically, Florence Lawrence became the first actress in films to acquire a nickname to *avoid* publicity. Lawrence became known and billed as the Biograph Girl in order to keep her real name off the screen. The idea really wasn't hers; it was Biograph's. The company wished to standardize their films as much as possible, and it didn't want its performers to become famous enough to make salary demands. This irked the nickelodeon fans of the early 1900s, who wrote in, demanding to know who the actors and actresses were.

In 1908 Carl Laemmle gave Florence Lawrence her earliest identification—and changed her nickname to the Imp Girl—after

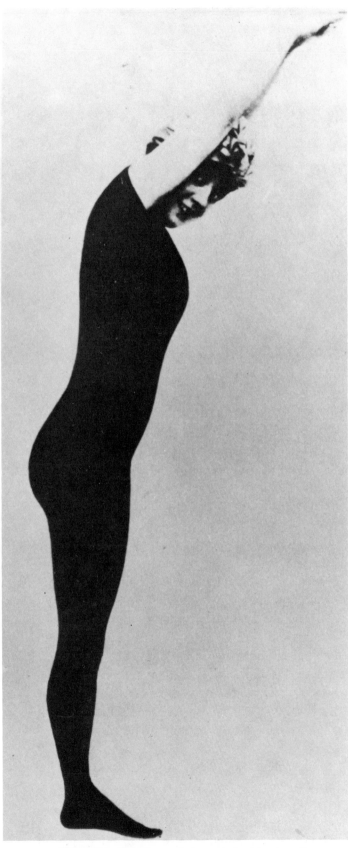

This swimsuit style was first popularized by Annette Kellerman, but that didn't stop MABEL NORMAND from posing in one.

luring her away from Biograph to his Imp Company. Fans finally found out who "the little girl with the golden curls" was, and Hollywood's star system had begun its first toddling steps toward dominating the motion-picture budget.

The Vamp

The first major publicity campaign designed to create a movie star gave America Theda Bara, the Vamp. Her screen name was catalogued as an anagram for Arab Death. She rode about in a death-white limousine attended by Nubian footmen. In Chicago she gave a press interview in an almost darkened room fully draped in black velvet, the air heavy with the musky aroma of incense. She shared most of her publicity photos with death symbols, skeletons, snakes, and other popular symbols of evil. Her photos also featured an ample display of leg and other assorted delights of the feminine form.

Introduced as the *femme fatale* in the screen adaptation of the stage play *A Fool There Was,* she went on to star in four dozen films. A line she spoke in a film (flashed on the screen on a title card in these silent-film days) became a favorite quotation for an entire generation. The line: "Kiss me, my fool!"

She was always the Vamp. To ask Theda Bara to portray a person who was not evil would be tantamount to asking Shirley Temple to enact the role of a sex goddess. Before she completed her contract with William Fox around 1918, her title was truly a household word.

Publicity stories acclaimed her as the daughter of a French father and an Egyptian mother; she bravely defended her background against a taunting press corps and more than one informant who remembered her as Theodosia Goodman, a movie extra from Ohio.

Nevertheless, Theda Bara's awesome success fostered a veritable horde of self-styled vamps who slunk onto the screen to try to take the spotlight from her. None proved successful; by 1918, a vamp could no longer lure the moviegoers. The beautiful vampires motivated by forces of evil to beckon and destroy a willing male by the merest flick of a finger or eyebrow had fallen out of public favor.

The Keystone Girl

Unlike Florence Lawrence, who hid behind her label as the Biograph Girl, Mabel Normand luxuriated in the fame and attention accorded her as the Keystone Girl. She was one of only two stars in the Keystone stable (Charlie Chaplin was the other) who ever emerged from Mack Sennett's madcap comedy performers as stars on their own.

A former fashion model, Mabel was brought into the movies by De Mille and made her screen debut for Biograph. When she moved over to Keystone, she slipped into snug, curve-revealing black tights and appeared prominently in the 1912 Sennett film *The Water Nymph.* The bathing-beauty look remained with her as she became the star attraction among Sennett's immortal Bathing Beauties. She was also a magnificent comedienne, truly the clown princess of the Sennett lot—and, if we can believe the gossip tales of those days, the apple in the eye of her boss.

Unfortunately, scandal was always a continuing threat to any movie actor or actress, and Mabel's illustrious career fell prey to a double-barreled explosion of notoriety that took her off the screen. First, the mysterious and still unsolved murder of director William Desmond Taylor drew both Mary Miles Minter and Normand into tabloid headlines. Both were key participants in the Taylor murder investigation; Minter was burdened with the indiscreet letters of love and passion she had penned to the director, and Normand, with Mack Sennett standing steadfastly behind her, was cleared of any connection with the crime.

Not long after that, Mabel brought her chauffeur to a party at the home of Edna Purviance, Chaplin's leading lady, and the chauffeur proceeded to put a bullet into another male guest.

A second scandal proved too much. Her notoriety brought her banishment from the movies, and many of her films were withdrawn from the screen.

But before these events terminated her career, Mabel Normand was a very, very special star of films about whom we will learn more later when we take a long, lingering look at Mack Sennett's Bathing Beauties.

Neptune's Daughter

Recruited from the vaudeville stage, where her specialty act was diving into and swimming around a tank of water on stage while clad seductively in tight black tights from ankle to waist and an equally form-fitting bodice up to the neck, Annette Kellerman came into films in a thinly disguised documentary that displayed her exquisite shape more vividly than the physical-culture exercises she demonstrated in the screen short subject.

If there was one thing Kellerman brought to the screen that most pleased the male moviegoer, it was the one-piece bathing suit. But even before that, Annette had gone even further with what must be termed the no-bathing-suit look. This was in *Neptune's Daughter,* the film story of a mermaid's transformation into a complete woman. On the screen she wiggled her hips and posterior delightfully to show off the finny half of her body. Then, maneuvering onto some sea rocks, she combed her long, very blonde tresses to cover her breasts and lap while early movie magic made the fishtail disappear, revealing a gorgeous female in unadorned splendor, scampering coyly among boulders that managed to hide some of the delightful anatomy that remained unconcealed by her flowing coiffure. The wolf whistles of 1914 shared the sound with the piano player in theaters where *Neptune's Daughter* played.

I was a brief part of the filming of one of her many movies, and it gave me one of my most provocative recollections of movie mermaids.

This Kellerman film was being made on location at Santa Cruz, an island off the central California coast, and—to put it in proper terms—things had not been going swimmingly with the production. We were two weeks behind schedule, and costly problems obviously nettled the studio's production headquarters. In those days I fancied myself something of a Lothario, a gent who today might be called a swinger. Anyway, that's how I remember me. I spent a lot of my time and money on fancy clothes, but most of all I was hung up on fancy automobiles. I owned a veritable fleet of sleek foreign roadsters in those days, and my racy cars served as my trademark.

That's why Fox studios called me one day. One of their production executives had to catch the boat to Santa Cruz in the morning, and I, the Hollywood gadabout with the fastest wheels in town, had been tabbed to speed him to the pier in Santa Barbara. Speed laws were as rare as good roads in those days, so I had the production exec at the boat dock well ahead of sailing. As the boat carried us toward Santa Cruz, he explained his mission: to speed up the location filming and get the company back to the studio, where work could continue at a faster pace amid the blessings of studio facilities and conveniences and under the watchful eye of budget-conscious production bosses.

It didn't take a genius to see what the trouble was. Lots of beautiful young girls in the cast, all playing mermaids, wearing fishtails, long hair, and very little else. They outnumbered the crew, three to one. All day long the film crew gazed on these darlings. And when the fading light halted the cameras, it was back to the tent city that had been erected to house the company. The dinner meal was over early. No movie theaters, no saloons or bars, no telephones, no newspapers or magazines. Sixty lovely, healthy girls. Twenty-four men of the film crew.

What to do? Please don't ask.

My passenger from the production department went into conference with the director and his assistants. Maybe this scene could be eliminated; perhaps this one could be filmed at the studio. This sequence might be shortened. Bit by bit they pared the schedule for an early location departure.

Next morning the cast and crew were informed of the shortened location schedule and early departure for home, and the mermaids wiggled their prop tails in disappointment. Incredibly, the exhausted crew broke out in cheers. It sure didn't take a Lothario with a fast roadster to understand their emotional reactions.

All I can say is that I sure as hell wished I could have been the still man on that picture!

Cutie Beautiful

Cutie Beautiful was the tag pinned on Clarine Seymour by someone on D. W. Griffith's staff. She was a dancer who had shown off a pair of very shapely gams in a musical number that had her whirling about in a grass skirt of the South Seas.

I was working for Griffith in those days. The big fashion news of that year for milady was the hobbleskirt. These skirts were snug around the ankles, prompting short, mincing steps. The streetcars—the great red cars of the Pacific Electric—ran by Griffith's studio then, and when Cutie Beautiful climbed aboard the P.E. to head for home, it was an event of the day. The word would go around that Clarine was headed for home, and a half dozen of us would nearly fall out the window, watching her lift high that hobbleskirt to maneuver the high step into the streetcar. I'm sure she knew we were watching, because she always did the skirt hiking with a flair.

You can have your look at next month's gynecological inspection of a girl's private parts. Give me one more look at Cutie Beautiful climbing aboard a streetcar.

The Girl with the Bee-stung Lips

Mae Murray had great legs, and she didn't mind showing them, but her lips were what made her famous. Mae had one of the most unique trademarks in the movies. Everyone knew her as the Girl with the Bee-stung Lips. I never thought her painted lips were all that attractive, but I must admit they were effective. Mae became a top star and remained one for many years. In 1924 Dorothy Mackaill painted on bee-stung lips for her role in *The Next Corner,* and hers were even more extreme than Mae's. I'm sure that didn't sit well with Murray, who felt that makeup style was her exclusive domain.

America's Sweetheart

It may seem incongruous to include America's Sweetheart, Mary Pickford, in a treatise on leg art—but doggone it, Mary had pretty legs! For almost a quarter of a century, the pretty girl with the long blonde curls dominated the screen. In 1919, when she married Doug Fairbanks, the movie fans of the entire world cheered and wept for joy. During that same year the famous newlyweds, together with Charlie Chaplin, helped create United Artists, prompting one unimpressed studio mogul to remark: "The inmates have taken over the asylum."

Mary never willingly posed for leg art, to my knowledge, but those little-girl outfits she wore on the screen were inevitably short, and even those white stockings couldn't completely disguise her shapely gams.

She did star in a dancing film, *Kiki,* in 1931, in the early days of the talkies, but my only recollection of her in a musical sequence of that film showed her hoofing in a man's tailored tuxedo, her long golden curls replaced by a very mannish haircut. Two years after *Kiki,* she starred with Leslie Howard in *Secrets*; then she announced her retirement.

The Girl with the Dimpled Knees

No showman ever did more to glamorize beautiful girls than Flo Ziegfeld, and one of his gorgeous showgirl stars was Ann Pennington. A dazzling beauty, Ann had something else— pretty dimpled knees. In fact, publicity about the dimples in her knees was so profuse that other exquisite portions of her superb anatomy were bypassed in deference to those famous joints.

Pennington was a Ziegfeld girl who eventually matriculated to the movie screen. Others recruited from the casts of the Ziegfeld Follies were Mae Murray and Lilyan Tashman.

The Platinum Blonde

An enterprising publicist, Lincoln Quarberg, pinned the tag *Platinum Blonde* on Jean Harlow as a gimmick to publicize Howard Hughes's 1930 movie *Hell's Angels.* Sound was still fairly novel in those days, and Harlow was never known as a paragon of elocution perfection, but no one (especially the men) forgot a line that Harlow spoke in the film: "Pardon me while I slip into something more comfortable."

Jean Harlow went on to become a true goddess of the movie screen, and throughout her fabulous career she never lost sight of the fact that showing off her figure in leg art was a definite asset to her popularity.

She has never been credited as the cause, but Harlow contributed more than her share— on the screen, that is—toward helping to bring about movie censorship and the Production Code administered by Will Hays. In fact, when the toughened attitude toward movie morals was adopted, Harlow was at MGM, starring in a film titled *Born to Be Kissed.* The movie was immediately rechristened *100% Pure,* but when it was finally released, it had become *The Girl from Missouri.*

During this period, the team of Clark Gable and Jean Harlow had provided the screen with some provocative, sex-adorned films that came to a halt with Harlow's unexpectedly sudden death. Many years later, Marilyn Monroe was to make her movie debut and inspire multitudes to exclaim, "It's Jean Harlow all over again!" In many ways their lives were curiously similar, from the sex-symbol identification through some highly scandalous romances, finally to deaths that cut short careers that were far from over.

The Goddess of Love

Six months before the Japanese made their sneak attack on Pearl Harbor, *Life* magazine came out with a photo of Rita Hayworth perched on a bed, clad in a scanty negligee, and proceeded to name her the Goddess of Love of the 20th Century. That picture of Rita proved to be worthy competition for the celebrated leg-art shot of Betty Grable that became the number-one pinup photo of World War II. When the atom bomb was dropped on Hiroshima, there were strong rumors that this pin-up pose of Hayworth was emblazoned on it. Whether true or not, by the time the Korean conflict erupted, Columbia studios were receiving several thousand letters a week, all asking for pinup shots of Rita.

Rita was a dancer, and she came from a dancing family, and she never had any objection to showing her gorgeous attributes. She had danced with her father on stage and, as Rita Cansino, had come to 20th Century-Fox in the thirties as a stock girl, hoofing in many of Zanuck's early musicals. When she eventually moved over to Columbia, she received a new last name and starring roles that brought her everlasting fame.

During World War II, she often appeared at the Hollywood Canteen, entertaining GIs. Dressed in the revealing tights of a showgirl, she would climb into a box and allow her husband, Orson Welles, to saw her in half as a highlight of his very popular magic act.

Later, she was to earn another title, princess,

RITA HAYWORTH in the 1945 Columbia movie *Tonight and Every Night.*

when she married Ali Khan, son of the Aga Khan. Rita was thus a titled lady considerably before Grace Kelly became the Princess of Monaco with her marriage to Prince Rainier. But she was not Hollywood's first authentic royal title. Before Pola Negri ever arrived in the movie capital, she was a countess as a result of her marriage to a Polish count whom she divorced prior to her introduction on movie screens. During the heyday of the feud between Pola and Gloria Swanson, "Countess Dombski" perhaps nettled Gloria as much as "Pola Negri." Whatever the inspiration, Swanson soon married the Marquis Henri de la Falaise de Coudray and thereafter sent out party invitations as Madame la Marquise. Hollywood's first legitimate princess, though, was Mae Murray, who acquired the title with her wedding to Prince David Mdivani of Russian Georgia. The marriage-go-round continued when Negri, after her great romance with Valentino, married Prince Serge Mdivani and eventually became both an ex-countess and an ex-princess, a Hollywood "record" that still stands.

The Sweater Girl

I suppose it might seem strange for me to talk about Lana Turner's legs in view of what she accomplished for the sweater, but the unvarnished truth is that Lana had—and still has—a great pair of super-pins. I know that for a fact, because I photographed those lovely limbs on more than one occasion; in fact, I was among the first motion-picture photographers to do a portrait sitting with Turner.

Just to set the record straight, Lana Turner was not discovered sipping a soda in Schwab's Drugstore. It happened at least two miles east of Schwab's but still on Sunset Boulevard, at a student hangout across the street from Hollywood High School, which Lana was attending. Her discoverer was the editor and publisher of the trade journal *The Hollywood Reporter,* with main offices a half block down

LANA TURNER in mid-career.

the street. W. R. "Billy" Wilkerson knew sex appeal when he saw it, and Lana Turner, even in her teens, was sex appeal personified.

I first met Lana after Billy Wilkerson called the famous Warner Bros. producer and director Mervyn Leroy, to tell him about the gorgeous girl he had discovered. Soon thereafter, Mervyn called me and asked me to take photographs of the pretty girl who was destined to dominate the movie screens with her dazzling beauty, her fabulous body, and—let's never overlook this—her great talent as an actress.

I told Mervyn Leroy that I would reserve time at the studio portrait gallery and arrange the photo session.

"Oh, no, not that!" Mervyn cut in hastily. "Shoot her someplace else—away from the studio!"

Mervyn was not about to cross swords with Jack Warner over an untested girl who wanted to break into the movies. If Warner discovered that one of his executives was planning to place someone on a personal contract without reference to the studio, the fur would really fly. Secrecy was a must.

"Why not shoot her at home?" Leroy suggested.

I followed his orders and went to Lana's place—a fairly unpretentious abode, as I recall—and spent an afternoon photographing her. Just portraits, head shots. Sure, I easily discovered that she had a sensational figure, but Mervyn had said portraits, and that's all I took. Now, *that's* what I call a faithful employee!

Quite possibly these were the first studio photos ever taken of the woman who soon became the most photographed star in Hollywood, but of course, they never saw the light of publication at that time. Quite a bit later, however, I loaned the negatives to Lou Valentine of Time-Life, and he had a set of prints made. Lou and Mervyn Leroy have the only copies of Lana Turner's first portraits, as far as I can learn. I still have the original

negatives, of course. Jack Warner doesn't have any.

Getting back to Lana's well-filled sweater—when she first got a chance to appear in a movie (it was a Mervyn Leroy film), the world-famous bosom missed the spotlight. Instead, it was a shot of her legs and fanny that dominated the screen in a scene showing her walking away from the camera. A great scene it was, too!

The Sarong Girl

Dorothy Lamour's first title was Miss New Orleans as a result of a beauty contest in 1931, but she is best known as the Sarong Girl, as a tribute to the exotic costumes she wore as a film star.

Dorothy entered the movies in a film titled *Jungle Princess,* but not until two years later did her performance for Paramount in *Typhoon* prompt that studio's praisery to dub her the Sarong Girl.

Even after her many screen successes as the female member of a great comedy-and-music triumvirate—Bing Crosby, Bob Hope, and Dorothy Lamour—in the popular "Road" movies, Lamour had not shaken her identification with the dress mode popular with both men and women in islands of the Pacific and the Malay archipelago. Even today as she dwells in semiretirement, she is frequently in print as the actress who brought world fame to the sarong.

She did more than popularize the sarong, however; she also altered it considerably. The authentic sarong began at the waistline and traveled down to the ankle. But movie censors had not yet got to the point where they would accept bared breasts on screen (and I'm sure Lamour hadn't reached that plateau of acceptance either). As a result, Dorothy's sarongs moved northward to cover the bosom. But there was consolation in another change in the sarong that she wore. It was slit up the sides, much like a Hong Kong cheongsam, revealing much more dazzling leg art than the Pacific islanders ever supplied.

The Oomph Girl

In my more than fifty years around movie sets, I can count on the fingers of one hand the feminine stars who were also great gals. Barbara Stanwyck was one. And Carole Lombard. And of course, Joan Blondell. And then there was Ann Sheridan.

Annie was very special. Her great and lasting fame never ruffled her feathers, and on that terrible day when a malignancy took her away from us she was still the same honest, unspoiled, fearless, down-to-earth, beautiful creature she had been before the movie camera exposed her rich talents and gorgeous good looks to carry her to international idolatry.

DOROTHY LAMOUR celebrates New Year's Eve among the bubbles in a champagne glass.

ANN SHERIDAN showing off her gorgeous legs in the costume she wore in Universal's 1953 film, *Take Me to Town,* opposite Sterling Hayden.

65

By the time Ann Sheridan showed up at Warner Bros., I was already well ensconced at that studio. Warners always kept a rich stock company of great stars in those days—Cagney and Flynn and Blondell and Bogart and Alan Hale and Allen Jenkins; the list goes on and on—and its still gallery was feverishly grinding out as many photographs of the many stars and starlets as was humanly possible. I was working with such fine Hollywood photographers as Burt Longmore and Scotty Welbourne, and the demand for leg art was so great that we often erected a temporary still gallery on a sound stage in order to supply the leg-art market.

During the Warner musicals we covered the dance rehearsals too, and the minute there was a break we whisked the chorines into our makeshift photo studios and began clicking away. We also covered the stars in offstage shots, some candid, some specially posed. Marion Davies, Joan Blondell, and Ruby Keeler were among those who faced our cameras at Warners.

Very few of the feminine stars resisted leg art. They were contract players, and they worked for Jack Warner, and they took their orders from him. If Warner approved a contract actress as a cheesecake subject, she posed. Today's stars, male and female, dictate what they will do and what they won't do. They couldn't have done that in Warner's regime.

Don't call it glamour slavery. It was the nature of the film industry. Studio tycoons decided who would become film stars. Then they simply made them stars. Big stars. Lasting stars. A few more studio tycoons around today, men who knew what they were doing and fearlessly went about doing it, could well be the salvation of an industry that seems to be deteriorating into an aimless, milling throng of individual moviemakers proceeding without the discipline of management control and armed with the enormous resources of outside industries far removed from films but seeking the benefits of tax shelters, write-offs, and capital gains.

Ah, but that's a different soapbox.

We were concerning ourselves with something much more pleasant: Ann Sheridan.

Annie, as any movie buff will tell you, became the Oomph Girl, hated every single letter of that trademark, but lived up to every inch of the title that had been circulated to make her famous, to create a new star for the screen.

A member of the Warner Bros. publicity staff, Bernie Williams, who worked as art director of the still department, was the man who originated the Oomph Girl title for Sheridan. From that day forward she wore it bravely but without pride. We didn't help her much, either. We stopped calling her Annie and began to call her Oomphy.

Leg art of Sheridan as the Oomph Girl poured out of the studio faster than water over the ledges of Niagara. George Hurrell, one of Hollywood's most respected freelance portrait photographers, took the first ''Oomph'' stills of Ann for *Esquire*. Meanwhile, at the studio Scotty Welbourne and I were shooting away as the publicity mill invented ways to define oomph pictorially. On one occasion Scotty and I were shooting Annie in a full rack of specially designed oomph costumes, and Sheridan was posing and changing as quickly as she could. At one point she delayed her appearance from the dressing room much longer than we thought necessary. Scotty and I had set the lights and arranged the chaise longue on which she was to recline in seductive repose.

''Okay, Oomphy, we're ready!'' I called.

No response.

''Having trouble?'' I inquired.

Again no response.

''You still in there?''

Silence.

I was just about to enter the dressing room and investigate, when Annie finally communicated with us.

''Get set for something special,'' she hollered, and made her entrance clad in the grubbiest suit of winter underwear I ever saw, a pair of long johns that had conceivably outlived the Gold Rush.

"Okay, experts," said Annie, "let's *see* you make *this* look oomphy."

I sure wish we'd tried to do what she said. Those photos would be collector's items today.

Ann Sheridan was not only friendly, but she was faithful to her friends. We were close pals, and she never failed to ask for me as still photographer whenever she began a new film role. Occasionally a conflicting assignment might prevent it, but I shot the stills on almost every movie Annie made.

I remember well when she was starring in *King's Row* and Warners' publicity director sent down a note: "Get leg art of Sheridan—right now." Well, *King's Row* was a period film, and the costumes were very full and about as revealing as a pea-soup London fog. I showed Annie the memorandum.

"Got any ideas?" she asked.

I shook my head.

"Well, if you come up with something, let me know," she added, and disappeared into her portable dressing room.

Later that afternoon I knocked on her door.

"I've got an idea for that leg art," I told her. "Can I show you?"

I led her to a prop tree standing in a corner of the sound stage. "Up there." I pointed.

"Sitting on a branch in thirty yards of skirt and petticoat?" Annie asked. "You call that leg art?"

"Not sitting," I suggested. "Hanging."

"Hanging!"

"Yeah, by your knees," I said. "Upside-down."

Sheridan stared at me as if I had just rolled back my eyeballs and foamed at the mouth.

"Look, Annie," I said, "there's no way to get leg art out of these costumes you're wearing, and that's what I told my boss on the phone, but he doesn't listen very well. I'm going to have to show him, I guess."

Sheridan didn't even bat a false eyelash. "Okay, Maddie," she said. "Get the

goddamned ladder."

Annie climbed up to the limb, got into position, and dropped down to hang by her knees from the branch. The skirt fell, completely concealing her identity, and the layers of petticoats only added to her anonymity. All that could be seen were her heels and her black bloomers. I clicked away merrily, then rescued her from the tree.

The next day I sent the proofs of Sheridan hanging upside-down in the tree with a note identifying the shots as the leg art requested. As inconceivable as it may seem, I never heard a word about those stills. That disappointed me. Not only had I supplied him with leg art—but I had given him a choice of limbs!

The Ping Girl

Don't ask me how Carole Landis became known as the Ping Girl, because I wasn't present at the christening. But I worked with Carole, and I can assure you from firsthand experience that the shapely figure of Landis could make any redblooded male go "Ping!" or "Bong!" or even "*Zowee!*"

The beautiful blonde with the sensational curves came into the movies in 1937 as one of a flock of beauties in the Marx Brothers comedy *A Day at the Races.* Except for a few flings in the cinematic sagebrush in some Republic westerns and episodes of a serial, *Daredevils of the Red Circle,* Carole put her whistle-bait beauty on display in several musicals such as *Broadway Melody of 1937, Varsity Show,* and *Gold Diggers in Paris.* Not until late 1939 did her big chance come along, starring with Victor Mature in *One Million B.C.* while clad seductively in form-fitted animal skins. From that picture on, Carole became a big-name screen performer.

Her career matured in musicals, and she really learned how to strike a leg-art pose. Truly a photographer's delight, Carole racked up almost as much mileage in pinup photos as she did in motion-picture films. Matching

Carole's gorgeous gams were a magnificent chest and a callipygian posterior. One movie chronicler had been moved to describe her as "a bureau with the top drawer pulled out." From the time she hit it big in films until the tragic suicide that took her away, Carole Landis never forgot that leg art was important. Among the Hollywood glamour photographers, I never met one who didn't think she was someone very special.

But I still don't know how she made people go *"Ping!"*

The Body

Looking much younger than her years, Marie McDonald, a Kentucky doll, had first attracted attention in Hollywood as a female vocalist with the Tommy Dorsey band. She was then known as Marie Frye, and to look at her, no one would ever imagine that she had been a John Powers model and a member of the Broadway cast of *George White's Scandals.* Oh, she had the looks, all right, but her appearance was less like a New York model and showgirl and more like a high school student getting set to try out as a cheerleader.

Marie came into the movies in 1941. She appeared in such films as *It Started with Eve* and *Pardon My Sarong,* and although the title escapes me, I recall that she appeared in a United Artists release in which she played a girl known as the Body. Quite naturally, the publicity campaign on the film soon had bestowed on her the inevitable trademark.

In later years Marie McDonald found herself the slave to her publicity title, wishing, perhaps, that she had no body so she could retreat from her headlined identification. This was especially true when she put together a sensational nightclub act and became a Las Vegas supper-club hit. Marie was a fine, professional chanteuse, but to the Las Vegas visitor, the hotel-casino operators, and the blue-chip rollers, she was still the Body, and all her show-

A Busby Berkeley dancer at the age of fifteen, CAROLE LANDIS went on to become world famous as the Ping Girl.

68

biz costumery was carefully styled to show it off.

Marie "the Body" McDonald, a great favorite of the leg-art fanciers and photographers, had her ups and downs during a twenty-four-year career in films. Broken marriages (to actors' agent Victor Orsatti and to shoe magnate Harry Karl) helped provoke more than her share of personal disillusionment and discontent.

Her behavior on a few occasions was considered irrational by a few detractors. Insiders say she had turned to drugs to ease her melancholy. One of her constant boosters was the late Harrison Carroll, the celebrated Hollywood columnist of the *Los Angeles Herald-Express*. It's a fitting movieland anecdote that when Marie McDonald had purportedly been kidnapped, she managed to elude her captors and raced to a telephone. But her first call didn't go to the police or FBI; it was to Harrison Carroll!

On October 21, 1965, a drug overdose took the Body away.

The Sex Kitten

Many attractive and seductive ladies came along after Marilyn Monroe to lay claim to her throne as Hollywood's reigning sex symbol— Jayne Mansfield, Mamie Van Doren, Diana Dors, to name just three—but the most logical heiress turned out to be a mademoiselle from Paree by the name of Brigitte Bardot.

Both on the screen and off, Bardot went her sexy way to establish her international reputation as the Sex Kitten. She gave delighted male movie fans a bit more than usual to leer at on the screen, and perhaps more than any other film star of the late fifties and early sixties, Brigitte helped break down the barriers of cinema censorship. Undoubtedly, she also did her bit to help bring about such byproducts as the Motion Picture Code and the magazine centerfold.

Brigitte was posing for delectable leg art long

MARIE MC DONALD was known in films as *The Body*—and not without reason. Before her 1941 screen debut, she was a band singer for Tommy Dorsey under the name Marie Frye. She died in 1965.

69

before the movies discovered her. The magazine *Continental Film Review* featured her provocatively on many of its calendars and posters. Her fame came about as much via those magazines, posters, and calendars as from motion pictures.

When the public first sat up and took notice of BB, she was a teasing brunette in a skimpy bikini. Later, her tresses turned blonde, and her excellent figure was on display more revealingly than ever.

But Bardot was never really a bathing beauty in the true sense of the word. She had a very definite personality in photos, and her special traits were always on display. To put it another way, Bardot was much more cat than kitten. She represented a new breed of glamour girl—tough minded, free of moral restriction, untamed, earthy, and uninhibited. For instance, if Brigitte Bardot had posed for Fourth of July leg art, she would have been exploding the firecracker instead of riding on it.

But in the field of leg art she was a true princess. She had begun her career as a model, and she never forgot how to pose. And those challenging looks paired with her luscious curves combined to excite any male leg-art fan.

Even when the years began slipping by, Bardot maintained her whistle-bait looks. Later, however, she changed her character. The Sex Kitten discarded her animal-like traits and devoted herself to the protection of other animals. At the age of forty-two she organized the Animal Protection Foundation, but within three months the response was so great that she was forced to close it down, lest she be forced to devote all her time and most of her personal funds to administration demands. Brigitte failed to realize that when she snaps her fingers, the willing world immediately beats a path to her door, whether it's to save the animals of the world or to provide comfort to the world's greatest Sex Kitten.

The Polkadot Girl

The aspects were somewhat more commercial than usual when actress Chili Williams hit the magazines and newspapers as the Polkadot Girl. It was an all-out campaign, but it was meant to sell polkadot material more than Williams's budding screen career.

Chili Williams was a real looker; how fine an actress she might have been was never really proved, because her film roles were not big in quantity or quality. But a manufacturer of polkadot material thought she'd make a sensational salesperson for his wares. He provided her with an entire wardrobe—dresses, coats, slacks, bathing suits, dressing gowns, sleepwear, you name it—and every outfit was polkadot.

And, oh, how the Polkadot Girl stood out in a crowd!

Naturally, photographers had a field day pointing their cameras at the delectable Williams. And editors also rallied to her side with voluminous exposure of those sexy polkadot pictures. Chili Williams was truly a lovely leg-art lady. Every time I think of her, I get spots before my eyes.

The Face

Anatomical identification quite often moved hand in hand with screen beauty. However, not all the nicknamed dollies were necessarily leg-art lovelies. Anita Colby, a top New York cover girl, had a face that was unbelievably gorgeous. That face glowed on many magazine covers, and it was a foregone conclusion that one day her phone would ring and Hollywood would be on the other end of the line.

When she finally did come into films, press agents began thinking up a tag for her—and all of them came up with the same suggestion: the Face.

ANITA COLBY

Colby, whose brains were as impressive as her beauty, eventually wound up as a top agent. And during her acting career she rarely posed for true leg art. Photos of what went along with the Face are somewhat rare, but Anita was smart enough to realize that leg art was part of the movietown game. And anyone who ever saw a leg-art shot of Colby realized that the Face was not the whole story of this gorgeous gal's attributes.

The Look

Some time after the Face left films, we were treated to the Look. A famous look it became, too, and it belonged to another fashion model turned actress, Lauren Bacall.

Movie fans were introduced to the Look in a highly successful film, *To Have and Have Not,* produced during the war years and starring Humphrey Bogart. The film marked Bacall's debut, and from the moment she first appeared on the screen she was a true movie star. She not only won over millions of movie fans, but she also captured Bogart, who eventually married her, and their mating remained perfect right up to Bogie's death.

Lauren Bacall came about her nickname honestly. Anyone who can recall *To Have and Have Not* will never forget those lingering looks she aimed at Bogart. And for sure, they'll always remember those famous lines spoken by the Look: "If you want me, just whistle. You know how to whistle. Just pucker up your lips and blow."

LAUREN BACALL

MARLENE DIETRICH, who was Josef von Sternberg's discovery, appeared in many popular German and French films before coming to America in 1930 to begin a fabulous Hollywood career. Her performance as a saloon songstress with James Stewart in the 1939 film *Destry Rides Again* won her as many raves as her role as a cabaret singer in *The Blue Angel*. She warbled, "See what the boys in the back room will have." This delightful leg-art pose is from the 1948 movie *A Foreign Affair*.

...AND OTHER LEG ART LADIES

I'm quite certain that there were very few well-established stars of the motion-picture screen who would allow themselves to be identified as leg-art ladies. Nevertheless, there were a lot of them. Many leg-art ladies became actresses, and many actresses became leg-art ladies, whether by necessity or by choice. Some posed for leg art in order to become better known. Others posed for leg art only because a role they were portraying demanded it.

Theda Bara showed practically everything she had (and that was considerable!) because she was convinced it could make her famous. It did.

Conversely, the sight of the immortal Garbo clad in an abbreviated track suit, pretending she was a hurdler or a sprinter, seemed about as appropriate as a clergyman in an I LOVE LINDA LOVELACE T-shirt.

Each in her own way, Bara and Garbo qualify as leg-art ladies.

I have been meeting, working with, running into, promoting, establishing, even immortalizing leg-art ladies for more than a half century. I may have met one or two leg-art ladies whom I didn't like, but I can't think of a single one at the moment.

I knew a lot of leg-art ladies during those fifty-odd years (and they weren't odd years at all), and my memory bank is crammed with delightful recollections of most of them. But these remembrances, as I muster them out from the pages of my past, are on occasion blurred by time, grown hazy through the passing years, altered by the decades just as history is often altered by the erosions of time or the whims of the historian.

What I am trying to say is that my memoirs may include inaccuracies here and there, and if a reader chooses to prove me wrong, let him be my guest. I am not writing for the history books.

Carole Lombard never had one of those fancy nicknames, to my knowledge, but she was a classy leg-art lady. I worked on Carole Lombard movies only on a few rare occasions, but those assignments were enough to make me a dyed-in-the-wool, forever-and-a-day Carole Lombard fan. I guess I was always attracted to beautiful women who weren't really impressed by their own good looks. Carole was always a star who didn't act like one. It was easy to see how she became the number-one woman in the world for Gable. I know that if she had played her cards right, she sure as hell could have had me, too.

Lombard was never a stranger to leg art. In her early days in the movies she had worked for Mack Sennett and had appeared in Al K. Hall comedies and Century comedies. Gobs of gam photos were par for those courses. She knew how to pose, and she knew the value of good leg art. She was also careful to avoid bad leg art.

I especially recall one Lombard movie on which I was shooting the stills. The late Alex Evelove, who was later to become one of Warner Bros.' most gifted publicity directors, had been brought out from their New York offices to the West Coast studios in Burbank to work on productions as a unit publicist. His first assignment was this Carole Lombard film, whose title escapes me at this writing.

Alex Evelove always considered himself a good photographer, and on his first visit to the set he brought along his own personal 35-millimeter camera. Back in those days the unions were not as strong or as strict as they are today, and outside photographers were frequently allowed to come on the set and shoot their own photos. Evelove, on his first day, promptly aimed his camera at Lombard and started clicking away. A short time later, Carole called me over.

"Who's that jerk shooting pictures?" she asked me. Only she didn't say "jerk," because to Carole, a word like that would have rated as a church expression in her vocabulary, which could shake up an army sergeant.

I went over to Evelove, whom I had not yet met, and asked his identity.

"I'm the unit publicist," Alex informed me.

"That camera doesn't look anything like a typewriter," I replied. "Now, personally, I don't care whether you take any pictures, but it seems that Miss Lombard does."

Evelove stowed his camera, but he wasn't yet clear of trouble with Carole. A day or two later he came to the sound stage with eleven-by-fourteen enlargements of some of the photos he had taken of Lombard and proudly showed them to her.

Carole took them and slowly, carefully, one by one, tore each one into tiny pieces. Then, as the last bits of photo paper drifted to the floor, she called on her most colorful vocabulary and told Evelove precisely what he could do with the photos he hadn't shown her. As a red-faced Evelove departed the set, I glanced into the stage's butt-bucket where Lombard had deposited the ripped photographs. I swear, each little piece appeared to be singed around the edges. Well, the celebrated Lombard language was surely volatile enough to burn anything that crossed its path.

I'm sure that Alex Evelove eventually mended his fences with Lombard. She was never the sort to nurse a grudge for long. As I mentioned earlier, Carole was one of the three or four great all-around good sports who ever worked in motion pictures. The tragic airplane crash that took her away from the Hollywood scene provided the film industry with one of its saddest moments. Exciting feminine stars have come along since, lots of them, and I'm sure there will be many more in the future. But there will never, never be another Carole Lombard.

Million-dollar Legs

In show business there were quite a few pairs of legs that were worth a million dollars. That is, they were worth being insured for a million bucks. The first million-dollar insurance policy on gorgeous gams was made out to the French musical comedy star Mistinguette, who appeared with such as Maurice Chevalier in such Parisian revues as Folies-Bergère and Moulin Rouge for nearly five decades. Mistinguette's beautiful legs became a show-business legend of the flapper era. That was a nice period for legs, inasmuch as the bosom was being heartily deemphasized.

But the girl with the million-dollar legs whom I recall most vividly was Betty Grable. Certainly one special photo of Grable's legs eventually became the most famous leg-art photo the world has ever known.

Oh, there have been other famous leg shots, I know. Who can forget that picture of Marlene Dietrich's legs on full and welcome display as she posed languidly in her nightclub costume for *The Blue Angel?* Dietrich not only had sensational limbs; she knew how to show them to advantage. From her earliest days in German films as a *femme fatale* to more recent years when, as a glamorous grandma, she headlined shows in Las Vegas, she never lost sight of the fact that people still liked to look at great legs like hers.

Also, among the unforgettable leg-art photos of all time, we must not overlook that shot of Marilyn Monroe joyfully trying to keep her skirt under control as hot air from a manhole cover whipped it heavenward. The photo became the billboard for the movie she was making at the time, *The Seven Year Itch.*

Great shots they were, as was the sexy photo of Rita Hayworth spread out on a satin-sheeted bed, a leg-art special that made her the wartime pinup queen second only to Grable.

That famous Grable pose was a black-and-white photo that was later hand colored and reproduced after its immense popularity was assured. How that picture came to life bears repeating.

At the turn of the frantic forties, in the softly undulating hills of western Los Angeles, 20th Century-Fox studios was a veritable circus of activity as it ground out its annual allotment of sixty movies, some good, some bad, some unforgivable. Along the wide avenues of the film lot strode the conjurers and the clowns, the divas and the dancing bears, the rodeo artists and the ringmasters. Like windblown moths they fluttered to the music of a golden Pied Piper: Darryl Francis Zanuck.

On the main floor of the three-story administration building in an emperor-sized office done in his favorite color, green, the brilliant showman and aspiring polo player

The great French cabaret star MISTINGUETTE set an enviable mark. She remained a star for a half century in Europe and was the first of the show stars to achieve publicity by insuring her legs for a million dollars.

75

MARILYN MONROE

ruled his domain with a firm hand, swinging his cut-down polo mallet as he moved back and forth, calling the shots that were many more times right than wrong.

And at least once daily he descended his private stairway, which led directly from his inner sanctum to his private gymnasium, where he went through the ritual of workouts, rubdowns, and steambaths that kept him vigorous through his eighteen-hour workdays.

In this health emporium two stories underground, he would regularly lace on pillow-sized boxing gloves for a sparring match with one of his contract junior writers. From time to time he would slip through a jab or an uppercut, and the junior writer would openly wince and plead, "Hey, Chief, not so hard!"

Understandable, you say? Well, not when the junior writer happened to be the former welterweight boxing champion of the world.

What the hell, it was Hollywood, and a job was a job.

Due north of the subterranean athletic arena where the chief never knew defeat, the studio commissary, the Cafe de Paris, with its garish murals, was a diurnal mecca where the gods, goddesses, and go-fers who slaved at the moviemaking trade met at high noon. Here they watched and awaited Emmett, the tall, smiling black man in the towering chef's hat, as he pushed his glittering silver serving cart among the patrons, tending the wants of those craving the daily special. Challenging the artistry of the most flamboyant of waiters on the dining cars of the *Chief* and *Super Chief,* Emmett would perform his culinary wizardry on a prime rib roast, roast Long Island duckling, or some other equally succulent gourmet dish.

Little wonder that the industry always referred to 20th Century-Fox of those days as the Country Club.

A few short steps from the Cafe de Paris was a small, unimposing building that was a center for a different sort of movie magic. This was the 20th Century-Fox portrait gallery. Here the stars, big and small (except Will Rogers, of course), the hopefuls and the handfuls, the starlets and the harlots came to call and to pose and to be photographed on orders from "someone upstairs." In the minuscule dressing rooms behind the giant backing that separated them from the gallery itself, gorgeous women became even more ravishing as they got into or out of their clothes, had their makeup and coiffures caressed by experts, and slithered in front of the still cameras and lights for the sake of pure and sweet publicity.

Occasionally the phonograph purred a soft, symphonic sound. Sometimes it blared jazz. Depending on the mood being sought to inspire the subject, tempos went from rhumba to rhapsody, from Beethoven to Berrigan, from calypso to Crosby.

The music was definitely upbeat the day that 20th Century-Fox portrait artist Frank Powolny was aiming his lens at the bathing suit that barely constrained the delicious curves of Betty Grable. Eyes glued to ground glass, Powolny circled his subject, capturing her classic silhouette for posterity. He had reached a position that promoted the Grable derriere as the center of interest but hid her bubbling blonde good looks.

"Betty! Look at me!"

Without altering her body pose, Betty swiveled her head and looked at him.

Click!

The most famous single piece of leg art the world has ever known and loved had been born.

Betty Grable in her one-piece white bathing suit, arms akimbo, smile aglow, gorgeous gams rising from spiked heels, was on her way to the inside of a machinist mate's locker aboard an assault transport in the Pacific, a foxhole in the Bulge, a USO in Georgia, a backpack on the beach at Normandy, the bulkhead of a B-29 carrying bombs to Tokyo, and the forward command post of an army unit banked on the Rhine. Wherever the GI went during World War II, carrying the battle to the enemy, Betty Grable went with him.

And even farther.

In the tumult of war, as opposing forces advanced or fell back, the litter of battle remained behind to be picked up by others. Betty Grable's bathing-suit pose also found its way to a cave on a Japanese-held island, to bunkers of the Luftwaffe, and to ships of the ill-fated Mussolini fleet.

In view of this, it would be safe to assume that leg art can be assessed as a power and force of considerable magnitude. There is no way of ascertaining whether Betty Grable's photo ever won or lost a World War II skirmish—but you can bet your honorable discharge it helped. Someone who should have known better once said that the American GI fought for the flag, Mom, and apple pie. I say that the soldier, sailor, or marine who took a last longing glance at the Betty Grable photo before going into battle was fighting to get the damned war over so he could get home to a date with a girl who liked cheeseburgers and necking in the back seat, and had legs like Grable's. And that same GI, if he had known just how the Grable photo was made, would have devoted his nightly prayer to blessing Mom and Dad and Sis—and Frank Powolny for having the inspiration to yell: "Betty! Look at me!"

But whereas the leg art of Grable duplicated itself into everlasting fame, it unconsciously did a disservice to the phrase *leg art*. From the Betty Grable pose came a new word that invaded the dictionaries of the English-speaking world and turned *leg art* into a piece of antiquity. The word: *pinup*.

Today, of course, even *pinup* is old-fashioned. In the current era of let it all hang out, pretty-girl posings are divested of any and all body coverings, save an occasional thin gold chain or a gem of sorts, and the lascivious postures of the poses prove beyond doubt that modesty is now and henceforth as evident as a Roman cardinal at a briss.

Now it's the nude, the centerfold. Awesomely endowed maidens arrange themselves in all manner of anatomical contortions that allow the prying camera lens prime access to the most sacrosanct of regions. Pubic areas appear to dominate—in truth, to overwhelm—the scene. Feminine and masculine anatomies bounce off the magazine pages in unfettered abandon, leaving nothing to the imagination.

Top male stars such as Burt Reynolds (who did it with a fine sense of humor and good nature) pose for full-length portraits with only a well-placed hand for concealment. Leading movie teams such as Vera Miles and Kris Kristofferson flaunt their nude sexual acrobatics in front of movie cameras and girlie-magazine photographers. The movie leading lady of the show-all eighties who has not disrobed and paraded for public scrutiny is rare indeed.

It is a sterling tribute to leg art that it continues to command an audience, interest, and enthusiasm in the face of the promiscuous posings that are prevalent today. It is indeed heartwarming to know that there are still people out there who appreciate a well-turned calf, a dimpled knee, and a shapely thigh.

Let us hope that leg art, or at least the peekaboo photos of the past, can climb on the nostalgia bandwagon and enjoy a renaissance. Otherwise, where can we go from here? Good Lord, is it within the realm of possibility that the red-blooded youth of tomorrow will be getting his kicks over a collection of pretty-girl X rays?

Thank goodness I have always been, still very much am, and will continue to be for as long as I remain on this blessed earth a joyful, loving leg-art devotee. Take it from me, when it comes to beautiful leg art, the eyes definitely have it. Anyway, mine do.

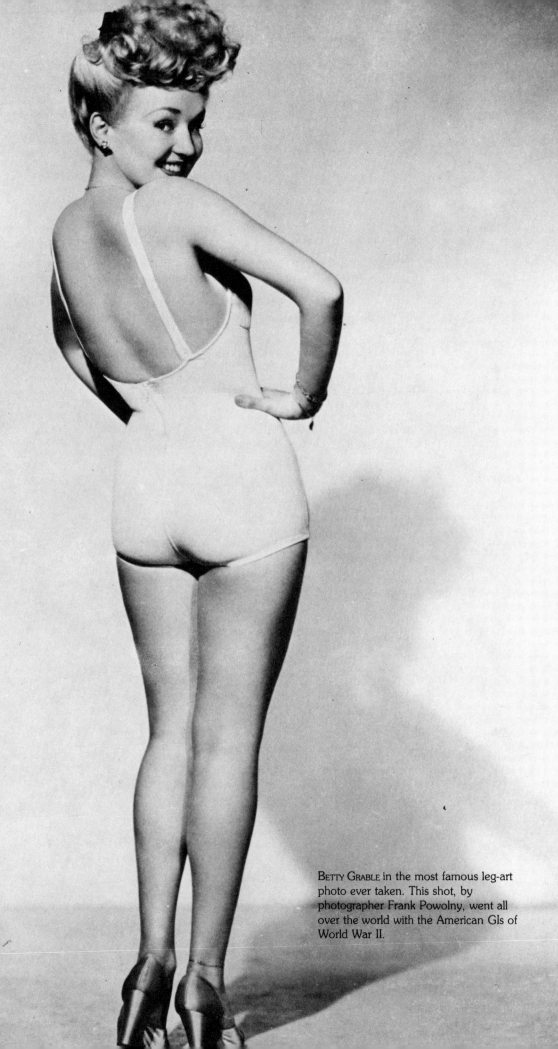

BETTY GRABLE in the most famous leg-art photo ever taken. This shot, by photographer Frank Powolny, went all over the world with the American GIs of World War II.

HARRIET HAMMOND, a Sennett Bathing Beauty, is posed beside the Pacific. It's doubtful that her swimming outfit ever got any closer to the water than this.

A GALLERY
OF LEG ART LADIES

A rare leg-art pose of Norma Shearer, who was Irving Thalberg's wife and the reigning queen of Metro-Goldwyn-Mayer. The diving board headstand is a scene from MGM's *The Women*, in which Norma starred with Joan Crawford and Rosalind Russell.

Barbara Stanwyck, one of the most durable of Hollywood's feminine stars, showed off her pretty legs in cheesecake poses such as this.

82

ROCHELLE HUDSON was a newcomer from Claremore, Oklahoma, when
Radio Pictures signed her to a contract.

A very early leg-art pose by the talented
performer DOROTHY SEBASTIAN.

JUANITA HANSEN, another pretty Mack Sennett Bathing
Beauty, dunks her toes in the Pacific at Santa
Monica's famous Castle Rock, in 1918.

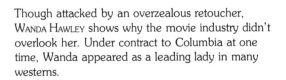

Though attacked by an overzealous retoucher,
WANDA HAWLEY shows why the movie industry didn't
overlook her. Under contract to Columbia at one
time, Wanda appeared as a leading lady in many
westerns.

A delectable gallery pose by the equally delectable poseur CARMELITA GERAGHTY.

ALBERTA VAUGHN, a delightful comedienne of the silent era, shows she has what it takes to make males leer as well as laugh.

Flanked by a bevy of MGM belles, ELEANOR BOARDMAN poses for a photo to publicize a movie called *Free Love*.

A leg-art shot of one of filmdom's fleeting starlets, DERELYS PERDUE, who shot into public notice and then disappeared.

BARBARA LA MARR became known as the girl who was too beautiful and went on to become a popular star of the twenties, but an untimely death cut short her career. Here, she is shown in a film scene with Ben Finney.

The movies were in their teens when aptly named ARLENE PRETTY posed so prettily. Arlene, who appeared in early serials and feature films, died in 1978 at the age of ninety-two.

EVA NOVAK may appear pictorially piscatorial, but how long, we wonder, did it take the photographer to put that fish on the hook?

RUTH CLIFFORD chose this pose to promote a movie career.

87

Long before she married Alan Ladd and became a well-known Hollywood actor's agent, SUE CAROL enjoyed success on the screen. Once under contract as a featured player at Radio Pictures, she appeared frequently on the screen opposite Buddy Rogers.

OLIVE ANN ALCORN was a Sennett beauty who probably had
oyster beds working overtime to produce her costume.

*Chateau Art
Studios
L.A.*

MARION DAVIES was not only the leading star of William Randolph Hearst's Cosmopolitan Productions, but she was also the apple of the publishing mogul's eye.

BEBE DANIELS was a silent star without stage experience who successfully bridged the awesome gap into sound pictures. She demonstrated her ability with dialogue and also unveiled a very pleasant singing voice.

A D.W. Griffith discovery, CAROL DEMPSTER kept time with the Dennis Shawn Dancers in the Babylonian sequence of Griffith's *Intolerance*. She later starred in several more films for the movie master.

LOUISE FAZENDA, the noted comedienne, proves there are laughs in leg art too. A great star for Mack Sennett, Louise later became the wife of film producer Hal Wallis.

89

HELENE COSTELLO made it a family affair when she joined her sister Dolores, under contract to Warner Bros.

A daughter of noted stage actor Maurice Costello, DOLORES COSTELLO was never a stranger to leg art. Before she became a screen star at Warner Bros., she danced on Broadway in *George White's Scandals*.

ANNA MAY WONG, a stunning oriental beauty and internationally popular actress, strikes a fetching pose for her role with Warner Oland and Sessue Hayakawa in Paramount's *Daughter of the Dragon*.

EDWINA BOOTH lent beauty and allure to many of Hal Roach's most popular comedies. Later she was to be fatally bitten by the tsetse fly during jungle filming of *Trader Horn*.

An unusual leg-art photo of MARJORIE RAMBEAU, who usually appeared on screen in more dignified poses. Marjorie had once worked in Alaska during the Gold Rush.

HELEN TWELVETREES, a star in RKO-Radio pictures, built a steady fan following as the tear-stained heroine who mourned the loss of virtue in those early talkie confession films.

Doesn't everyone have an ermine train like VIVIENNE SEGAL'S to slip into in case company arrives unexpectedly?

RUTH CHATTERTON is captured in a leg-art pose because a movie role called for it.

Seeing MAE CLARK and her gorgeous gams posed so prettily on a pedestal, it's difficult to understand why James Cagney would shove a grapefruit in her face.

PAULINE STARKE also successfully bridged the gap between silent and sound films, from Elinor Glynn's 1926 MGM movie *Love's Blindness*, opposite Adolphe Menjou, to the risqué scenes with Buster Collier in the 1930 film *A Royal Romance*.

CARMEL MEYERS was a silent-film star who was also featured on stage. Meyers struck this sultry pose between appearances in *Show Boat* at Hollywood's Pantages Theatre.

MARILYN MILLER, a great dancing star in Ziegfeld musicals, later came to Hollywood and Warner Bros. to star in *Sunny*.

"Swim for health," says COLLEEN MOORE as she poses on the diving board on the grounds of her palatial Hollywood home.

GERTRUDE SHORT was a chubby comedienne of the thirties but wasn't above showing off her legs and one of the world's most awesome beauty marks.

One of the early leg-art poses by CAROLE LOMBARD, taken early in her career when she appeared in Mack Sennett comedies.

As a Warner Bros. starlet, DOROTHY DEVORE utilized one of her shapely gams to welcome the Shriners to a Los Angeles convention.

Even the most dedicated movie buff might find it difficult to recall VIRGINIA BROWN FAIRE, but judging from this photo, it's nice that she dropped in on the movies, however fleeting her stay.

HOPE HAMPTON was a lovely leg-art lady who later married a wealthy industrialist and retired to a life of ease.

This may look like a carefully composed publicity photo, but it was actually a scene from a movie with LILLIAN LORAINE.

CLARA BOW dominated the sex appeal of the twenties, just as Harlow did the thirties. During that time, Clara was receiving more than twenty thousand fan letters a week.

A demure display for MARGARET LIVINGSTON, but still authentic leg art.

FAY LAMPHIER, giving leg art the old Annette Kellerman look.

LAURA LA PLANTE was much more attractive than this photo shows, but Laura was being mistreated by a photographer with little lighting knowledge.

When this photo was snapped, YOLA D'AVRIL was busy publicizing a Warner Bros. movie called *God's Gift to Women*.

A rare leg-art photograph of JANET GAYNOR. Janet looks as if she's actually planning to enjoy the water after the photographer has his day.

A rare leg-art pose by MYRNA LOY, one of the screen's most notable feminine stars. The draping was done with care because Myrna's limbs were somewhat heavy.

She was a highly popular comedienne, but WINNIE LIGHTNER had good legs and she didn't mind showing them.

Shortly after Mauritz Stiller brought GRETA GARBO to Hollywood and MGM placed her under contract, she ran the leg-art gauntlet by working out with the University of Southern California track team.

A very early leg-art pose by the unforgettable siren of sex MAE WEST. The "come up and see me sometime" gal came to the movies from a play titled *Sex*, which was considered the next thing to pornography.

In 1928 Nancy Torres was under contract to Universal.

Mary Duncan's costume revealed plenty as she starred with Sidney Blackmer in the 1930 film *Kismet*.

A great dancer, Gilda Gray starred on Broadway as the Shimmy Girl before Hollywood paged her in 1926 to play the title role in *Aloma of the South Seas*.

Leg art was strictly for laughs for Fanny Brice, the great Ziegfeld comedy star who was finally lured to Hollywood and the movies to make her film bow in Warner Bros.' *My Man* in 1928.

The celebrated Viennese beauty HEDY LAMARR wore considerably less than seen in this leg-art photo when she first electrified the screen with her revealing nude swim in *Ecstasy*. She was nineteen years old at the time.

ANITA LOUISE'S fresh blond beauty graced many of Hollywood's better movies. Here she is shown at a Santa Monica beach club.

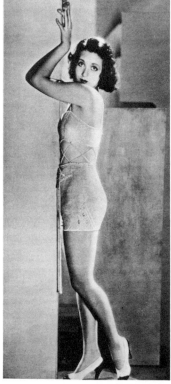

ANN SOTHERN was known as Harriet Lake when she posed for this photo.

MGM was making wonderful musicals shortly after sound arrived, and GWEN LEE was among the wonderful dancers who populated that wondrous world.

Rita La Roy, another portrait-gallery goddess, was a featured player under contract to RKO Radio.

Emerging from child to woman, ELIZABETH TAYLOR posed for this bathing-suit art at her favorite beach—the portrait gallery at MGM Studios in Culver City.

OLIVE BORDEN became a leading lady at Fox, appearing in such films as the 1927 movie *The Auctioneer.*

The normally auburn-haired PATSY RUTH MILLER becomes an alluring blonde in this boudoir shot.

MAY MC AVOY looks as uncomfortable posing for leg art as when she tried to continue her movie career as sound films came in. McAvoy, who lisped, had decided to forgo voice lessons because "my public would rather hear me speak in my natural voice." She sadly learned that the public didn't want to hear her speak at all.

ETHEL MERMAN wowed audiences on Broadway and in the movies, and she's a wow as a leg-art lady, too.

JOAN CRAWFORD as she appeared in a scene from MGM's *The Modern Age*.

PATSY RUTH MILLER strikes a provocative pose to publicize a Warner Bros. film, *The Aviator*.

British-born DOROTHY MACKAILL, a popular flapper star during the Jazz Age of movies during the twenties, emerged from a Flo Ziegfeld chorus line to become the reigning female star at First National, usually paired on the screen with Jack Mulhall. Dorothy made twenty-three talkies (her personal favorite was *The Barker*), and when she retired from films in 1937, she was quite wealthy, not from movie salaries but from real estate investments along Beverly Hills' famous Wilshire Boulevard.

When this engaging photo was snapped of SHEILA TERRY she was being featured with Loretta Young and George Brent in the provocatively titled *Week-End Marriage*.

Evelyn Brent was born Elizabeth Riggs in Tampa, Florida, and appeared importantly in films in both England and the United States.

Irene Hervey, who was the wife of actor Allan Jones, made her screen debut in 1933.

Genevieve Tobin had begun a stage career in 1919, moved on to films in 1931, and later became the wife of motion-picture director William Keighley.

Anita Page had been brought to MGM by Harry K. Thaw and was appearing in *Hollywood Revue of 1929* when this photo was taken.

Toby Wing, a well-known dancer with a gorgeous figure, was another screen personality who logged more footage in stills than on movie film. Here she is, under contract to Paramount in 1933.

The year was 1934, and Harriet Hilliard was singing with Ozzie Nelson's band every Tuesday and Thursday evening on CBS.

A dancer who appeared on the Broadway stage with Eddie Cantor in *Whoopee*, as well as in the later screen version, Eleanor Hunt eventually went under contract to Educational-Christie Comedies.

An accomplished dancer, June Knight appeared in many film musicals. At one time she was dancing as part of an act at the famous Coconut Grove of the Los Angeles Ambassador Hotel.

A Hollywood leading lady during those precarious days when movies went from silent to sound, Lila Lee was Lon Chaney's leading lady in *The Unholy Three*, the only talkie made by the *Man of a Thousand Faces*, which was completed shortly before his death.

Ruth King was appearing in the 1925 film, *The Devil's Circus*, when she posed for this publicity photo.

SISTERS G were twin showgirls who chose their unique professional name while dancing at Universal in the 1930 musical *King of Jazz*, starring Paul Whiteman and his orchestra.

NANCY KELLY, the well-known dramatic actress, appeared on Broadway in 1937 in *Susan and God* and came to 20th Century-Fox a year later to play feminine leads in such films as *Submarine Patrol, Stanley and Livingston,* and *To the Shores of Tripoli.*

FIFI D'ORSAY, one of the most popular and durable of all the French musical stars, enjoyed a long career in films as a dancer, singer, and comedienne. As late as 1972, almost fifty years after her career began, Fifi was still hoofing in a Broadway musical, *Follies*.

HEATHER ANGEL, an attractive British stage actress who came into films when the silent era ended, had an important role—and a fetching bathing suit for costume—in the 1933 Fox production *Charlie Chan's Greatest Case,* starring Warner Oland as the wily Chinese detective.

THELMA TODD is portrayed as a blond.

BENITA HUME was brought to Hollywood from London and made her MGM debut as Lee Tracy's leading lady in the 1933 movie *Clear All Wires.*

ALICE WHITE is shown here modeling a "daring" one-piece bathing suit. One of the great glamour stars of the late twenties, she was Clara Bow's biggest threat as jazz queen of the Flapper Era. Alice had appeared with Milton Sills in *The Sea Tiger*, played the ingenue lead in *The Private Life of Helen of Troy*, then exploded to stardom with Ruth Taylor in the 1928 Paramount hit *Gentlemen Prefer Blondes*.

This is a bona-fide leg-art photo of BENITA HUME, not a scene from a film.

ANNA NEAGLE, the piquant British star, is shown here as she co-starred with Ray Bolger in the 1941 RKO film *Sunny*.

MARIAN NIXON modeled this chic 1958 fashion style to help publicize her Columbia film *The Line Up*.

106

We're not sure whom MARY NOLAN is satirizing—probably Mary Pickford.

When this photo was taken, DOROTHY REVIER was appearing with Douglas Fairbanks, Jr., in the First National and Vitaphone production Sin Flood.

A very rare shot showing KAY FRANCIS's legs. She had great gams and a delightful figure but preferred to appear in films and photos as a dignified lady—which she was.

A rare shot of the great star MARY ASTOR, who lives out her years at the Motion Picture Country Home, writing another book to follow her autobiography, which caused a sensation in its day.

For twenty-five years JEAN ARTHUR reigned as a great Hollywood star. Jean didn't mind showing off her whistlesome figure. Back in the silents of 1925 she was doing small roles in Buster Keaton comedies. By 1928 she was a movie veteran of twenty-three, playing the feminine lead with the MGM comedy team of Karl Dane and George K. Arthur in Brotherly Love. In later years she triumphed in such screen classics as Mr. Deeds Goes to Town, You Can't Take It with You, and Shane.

NOEL FRANCIS, a former Ziegfeld Follies beauty, came to Hollywood to appear in the 1931 Warner Bros. film *Blonde Crazy.* This leg-art pose was captured while she was appearing in *Old Man Minick* starring "Chic" Sale.

A very sexy pose for CLAUDIA DELL. Claudia co-starred with cowboy hero Tom Mix.

The celebrated comedienne RUTH DONNELLY satirizes a leg-art pose for her role in Columbia's *The Amazing Mr. Williams.*

A talented musical star, DIXIE LEE, shown here in her role as a hula girl in Paramount's *Win or Lose*, went on to become Mrs. Bing Crosby. This is one of the few films she made after marrying Bing.

Few realize that beautiful ANNE SHIRLEY began making films in 1924 as a child actress, in *The Man Who Fights Alone*. She played the daughter of William Farnum and Lois Wilson. Her screen name at the time was Dawn O'Day.

108

A striking publicity photo, unusual for JEAN PARKER, who was usually seen as a sweet young thing in many MGM films of the early 30s. In the 1935 movie *Murder in the Fleet*, her leading man was a newcomer named Robert Tayler, who, one year before, had played a bit in a Jean Parker vehicle with Charles Bickford, *A Wicked Woman*.

One of two acting sisters, MARCELLINE DAY strikes a typical pose on the sands of Castle Rock on the beach at Santa Monica.

MAUREEN O'SULLIVAN, an Irish lass educated in a Dublin convent, came into films at MGM in 1931. One year later, her portrayal of Jane opposite Johnny Weissmuller's *Tarzan the Ape Man* exuded so much feminine charm that Louis B. Mayer handed her a long-term contract.

A nice leg-art pose by YOLA D'AVRIL to help publicize her role with Frank Fay in the Warner Bros.-First National comedy *God's Gift to Women*. D'Avril had also been prominently seen in MGM's 1930 movie *Those Three French Girls*.

IRENE DELROY, appearing in a 1930 film, *Nancy from Naples*.

An early leg-art photo of EDNA CONWAY by Autrey, the celebrated Hollywood glamour photographer.

An early leg-art shot of CONSTANCE BENNETT, who had been rising in film popularity when she married Phil Plant in 1926 and retired. Four years later, without a husband but with a million-dollar divorce settlement, she returned to Hollywood to become one of the great stars of the thirties, gaining legions of fans and followers in what were then known as confession films.

JOAN BENNETT, Connie's pretty sister, hit stardom in the early thirties. She is shown here in the aptly named role of Lazy Legs in a Universal murder mystery of 1945, *Scarlet Street*. Universal's partner in the film was Diana Productions, and Joan was Diana's vice-president and treasurer.

Everyone knew FAY WRAY as the favorite girlfriend of *King Kong* in the 1933 thriller. Here she is modeling beach togs on behalf of a Columbia movie, *Roaming Lady*.

This was a 1942 leg-art pose. Fan magazines had hailed ANN SHIRLEY's marriage to John Payne, tabbing them the ideal couple, but the mating lasted only six years. Ann retired from films at the age of twenty-six.

ALICE WHITE.

In the thirties at 20th Century-Fox, JANE WITHERS, shown here splashing in the pool at her Westwood home, posed a definite threat to Shirley Temple. In more recent years she became famous and earned a mint on TV for her characterization of a woman plumber.

111

OLIVIA DE HAVILLAND was a very young starlet when this leg-art picture was taken of her at Warner Bros., long before her triumphs in *Gone with the Wind, To Each His Own,* (an Oscar), *The Heiress* (a second Oscar), *The Snake Pit, Hold Back the Dawn,* and many others.

NANCY CARROLL was a Paramount star and won an Oscar nomination for her role in *The Devil's Holiday.* In 1965, Nancy Carroll died at age fifty-eight.

VIRGINIA MAYO in a 1954 pose.

LILLIAN ROTH came into the movies in 1929 at the same time that sound arrived, and her autobiography, *I'll Cry Tomorrow,* became an MGM screen hit with Susan Hayward in the lead.

VIRGINIA MAYO came into movies in 1944 and remained on the screen until 1967. She is the widow of actor Michael O'Shea.

Because VERONICA LAKE popularized a hair style that concealed one eye, she became famous as the Peekaboo Girl. Here's a photo of Veronica showing both of her eyes—and her legs.

MGM was AUDREY TOTTER's home for six years and fifteen movies. Her best role was as the star of *Lady in the Lake*, directed by and co-starring Robert Montgomery.

IDA LUPINO began her acting career as a sexy blond. Many years later she achieved great success as a screen director. In 1956 she announced her retirement as an actress, but in 1972 she resumed her acting career.

British-born blond beauty Lilian Harvey began her career in the early twenties, acting in German motion pictures. When this fetching photo was made, she was appearing in a Fox film, *My Lips Betray*, in 1933.

In films since 1948, Anne Francis worked mostly at MGM studios.

This lovely girl is Harlean Carpenter, who later became Jean Harlow.

114

BETTY GRABLE was a top-ten box-office star for nine straight years.

JOAN FONTAINE rarely showed her legs, but at one time she was a ballet dancer. This photo was for the 1937 RKO-Radio movie *Music for Madame*.

When this very early leg-art pose was taken, BETTY GRABLE was known as Frances Dean and was working in two-reelers at Educational.

MITZI GAYNOR entered films in 1950 and remained on the screen for nineteen years. A musical star of the supper-club circuit today, Mitzi still performs in an annual television musical special.

ALICE FAYE started making movies in 1934 and emerged as one of the greatest stars. Today she's married to Phil Harris, lives in Palm Springs, and is a very attractive grandmother.

LILY DAMITA worked in Hollywood during the late 1920s but was much better known as the wife of Errol Flynn than as an actress.

DOROTHY COONAN entered movies in the early 1930s and was the wife of director William Wellman for forty years.

One of the great durable stars of the movies, MARLENE DIETRICH has been appearing in films since 1930. She is shown here in the 1939 film *Destry Rides Again*.

116

MADGE BELLAMY, a screen actress
for fifteen years, scored a big hit
in the 1921 production of *Blind
Hearts*.

LOUISE BROOKS made films during
the silent era and switched
successfully to talkies. Her last
film was *Overland Stage Riders*,
with John Wayne, in 1938.

In films since 1934, IRIS ADRIAN
popularized the gum-chewing blond
wisecracker. Iris is still active in such
Disney films as *The Love Bug* and
The Apple Dumpling Gang.

In 1923, at the age of nine, JULIE BISHOP appeared in
Maytime. Until Warner Bros. signed her and changed her
name in 1941, she was known as Jacqueline Wells. This
photo is from the 1942 Warners movie *The Hard Way*.

117

VIRGINIA BRUCE, a stunning blond MGM star, was the wife of John Gilbert (1932–34), director J. Walter Ruben (1937–41) and Turkish playboy Ali Ipar (1946).

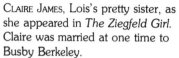
NATALIE MOOREHEAD.

CLAIRE JAMES, Lois's pretty sister, as she appeared in *The Ziegfeld Girl*. Claire was married at one time to Busby Berkeley.

LUCILLE BALL began her career in 1933 doing movie musicals.

A tap-dancing star who often appeared in films with Johnny Downs, ELEANORE WHITNEY retired from the screen in 1938, ending a three-year career.

The widow of Clark Gable and mother of his son, John Clark Gable, KAY WILLIAMS appeared in films during the 1940s.

119

CARA WILLIAMS, a gorgeous redhead, was once wed to John Barrymore, Jr. She also won an Oscar nomination for her supporting role in *The Defiant Ones*. This pose is from the 1956 film *Meet Me in Las Vegas*.

A 20th Century-Fox star of the thirties, ARLENE JUDGE had seven marriages and seven divorces.

BARBARA PEPPER began in films as a blond sexpot, then switched to character roles when obesity overtook her. This photo of Barbara, who died in 1969, is from the 1937 Joe E. Brown comedy *Wide Open Faces*.

120

LOIS JAMES, shown here in 1939 as an eighteen-year-old lovely posing for the Miss California beauty pageant.

A close friend of Ruby Keeler, singer WINI SHAW introduced the all-time hit tune, *Lullabye of Broadway*, in *Golddiggers of 1935*.

Aptly known as the Mexican Spitfire, LUPE VELEZ starred in a series of eight RKO films identified by that tag. In 1944, expecting an out-of-wedlock baby, she committed suicide. She was thirty-six.

From age two, HELEN PARRISH spent her life making movies, mostly in films with Deanna Durbin. She died at the age of thirty-five in 1959. This pose is from the 1941 movie *Too Many Blondes.*

MAUREEN O'HARA, as she appeared as *Lady Godiva* in 1955. Maureen's husband, Charles Blair, a former air-force brigadier general and the first solo pilot over the North Pole, was recently killed in an air crash. Widow Maureen lives at their home in the Virgin Islands.

LILY PONS, the French-born opera star, was in such films as *I Dream Too Much* (1935), *That Girl from Paris* (1936), and *Carnegie Hall* (1947).

JEAN PARKER came in to films in 1932 and appeared in sixty-eight movies over a thirty-four-year span. She retired shortly after the 1957 death of her husband, Robert Lowery, but recently announced her intention to return to the screen.

JANIS PAIGE, a Warner Bros. star of the forties, also starred on Broadway in *The Pajama Game.* Following the death of her Oscar-winning songwriter husband, Ray Gilbert, in 1976, Miss Paige returned to her acting career.

ELEANOR PARKER began in films in 1941. Among her memorable performances were Oscar-nominated portrayals in *Caged* and *Detective Story.*

122

This photo is from CLAIRE TREVOR's dancing role in the 20th Century-Fox movie about George M. Cohan, *Song and Dance Man*. An Oscar winner for *Key Largo,* Claire married film producer Milton Bren. She retired in 1965.

LUPITA TOVAR was in films from 1929 to 1945, but she is most widely recognized as the wife of Hollywood's superagent Paul Kohner and as mother of actress Susan Kohner.

LILYAN TASHMAN, a gorgeous blond who successfully bridged the gap from the silents to the talkies, was married to film star Edmund Lowe. She died in 1934 at the age of thirty-five.

The beautiful prima ballerina TAMARA TOUMANOVA was born in a Siberian freight car during the Bolshevik Revolution and became a dancing protégée of Pavlova, eventually going on to stardom on both stage and screen.

When MARIAN MARSH
appeared with Eddie
Cantor in *Whoopee*, she
was know as Marilyn
Morgan. Warner Bros.
changed her name and
publicized her as the First
Star of 1932, billed above
the title of a film called
Under Eighteen. But her
star career did not survive.

MERCEDES MC CAMBRIDGE's first movie, *All the King's Men*,
won her an Oscar. She was also nominated for an
Academy Award as a result of her fine performance in
Giant.

MGM starred the
beautiful blond
Hungarian soprano
ILONA MASSEY with
Nelson Eddy in
Balalaika. She retired in
1960 and died at age
sixty-two in 1974.

DOLORES MORGAN, a
promising Warner Bros.
starlet of the forties, was
married to film producer
Ben Bogeaus for fifteen
years. Her last movie role
was in the 1954 film *The
Silver Lode.*

124

MARIA MONTEZ was Universal's Technicolor
queen of the adventure fantasy. A native
of the Dominican Republic, she was
married to Jean Pierre Aumont. She was
forty-three when a bathtub accident
claimed her life in 1951.

MARJORIE MAIN was not a leg-art beauty, but she was an actress game for anything—including a song-and-dance role opposite Wallace Beery in MGM's *Jackass Mail.*

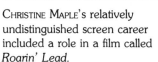

CHRISTINE MAPLE's relatively undistinguished screen career included a role in a film called *Roarin' Lead.*

A Spanish beauty, CONCHITA MONTENEGRO, came into American films in 1931. Her last American movie was *He Trusted His Wife,* in 1935. She was residing in Madrid when last heard from.

MONA MARIS, an Argentine actress who was once the wife of director Clarence Brown, appeared in United States films from 1929 to 1946.

125

Mary Jane Halsey was a pretty showgirl in Radio Pictures' *Rio Rita*.

In films since 1937, Ruth Hussey won an Oscar nomination for *The Philadelphia Story*. The wife of actors' agent Robert Longenecker, Ruth retired from films in 1960. This photo is from Columbia's *Our Wife*.

A United States Olympic team swimmer, Eleanor Holm sparked a scandal on board the ship carrying American athletes to Europe. She was the wife of showman Billy Rose for fourteen years and later married singer Art Jarrett. She now lives in Miami with her third husband, Tommy Whelan. Among her screen roles: Jane in the 1938 movie *Tarzan's Revenge*.

Jane Gilbert, the sister of Margaret Lindsay, appeared for Warner Bros. in *Invisible Stripes*.

Under contract to First National in 1930, LAURA LEE posed for this photo to publicize roles in *Top Speed* and *Going Wild*.

In movies since 1930, MARGOT GRAHAME gave a stunning performance in *The Informer*. She gave up her screen career in 1957. This photo is a fashion still from Columbia's *Counterfeit*.

DIANA LEWIS, shown here posing for wartime Christmas art, was known to filmgoers as Mrs. William Powell—and to Powell as Mousie. After making *Cry Havoc* in 1943, she retired. She now makes her home in Palm Springs.

RITA GAM was an apt name for a leg-art lady. Rita came into films from the New York stage. She was once married to film director Sidney Lumet.

BETTY LAWFORD, a British actress, usually portrayed aristocratic rich girls in Hollywood movies. She was Mary Boland's daughter in *Secrets of a Secretary*.

An ingenue who wore her hair in the style of Ann Harding, JEANETTE LOFF appeared in youth films of the late silents and early talkies. She cavorted with Paul Whiteman in *The King of Jazz*. She was thirty-six when she died in 1942.

Posing in a fashion photograph publicizing *The House of Seven Gables* for Universal, MARGARET LINDSAY made more than a hundred movies in a career that spanned thirty-one years.

PRISCILLA LANE was the youngest of the Lane sisters, and appeared in such films as *The Roaring 20s* and *Brother Rat*. She is retired and now lives in New Hampshire with her wealthy building contractor-husband, Joseph Howard.

A former New York artist's model, PATRICIA LAWSON came into films during the thirties. This leg art is in the 1936 style.

RUTH TERRY sang at the Chicago World's Fair, came to the movies in 1937, and was featured in such films as *Hold That Co-ed*, *Pistol Packin' Mama*, and *Three Little Sisters*.

129

ROSEMARY LANE was one of the famous Lane sisters of show business that also included Lola and Priscilla. Rosemary played Dick Powell's girl and the sisters sang with Fred Waring's orchestra in *Varsity Show*. Prior to her death in 1974, Rosemary was a Southern California real estate agent.

JOAN LESLIE played Mary, the girl Jimmy Cagney sang about in *Yankee Doodle Dandy*. Most of her screen roles characterized the girl-next-door.

An unusual photo of GYPSY ROSE LEE, the great striptease star, who shows only her legs here. When she was brought to films by Darryl Zanuck, movie censors forced her to change her professional name to Louise Hovick.

LOIS LINDSAY, one of the famous Busby Berkeley beauties in *Gold Diggers of 1933*, is the widow of Madison Lacy, author of this book.

130

A leg-art pose for ANN SOTHERN'S starring film *Swing Shift Maisie*, a World War II screen favorite.

The great singing star of the Metropolitan Opera GLADYS SWARTHOUT starred in four film musicals during the late thirties. She died in 1969 at the age of sixty-four.

Another great Met opera star, RISË STEVENS costarred in 1941 with Nelson Eddy in MGM's *The Chocolate Soldier*. Today she's head of New York's Mannes College of Music.

MAUREEN O'SULLIVAN is shown modeling a bathing suit for a fashion layout. Maureen was the most famous of all the Janes appearing on screen with the many Tarzans. She's also famous as the mother of screen star Mia Farrow.

131

One of the truly heavenly bodies of show business, MARIE WILSON had a forty-one-year career as an actress and comedienne. She starred in *Boy Meets Girl* in 1938 and later played the title role in *My Friend Irma*. During seven years in the forties on stage with Ken Murray in *Blackouts*, in Hollywood, Marie never missed a single performance. She was fifty-six when she died in 1972.

VERA ZORINA was born Brigitta Hartwig. She danced with the Ballet Russe de Monte Carlo in the early thirties and on screen to the tune of ''That Old Black Magic'' in *Star Spangled Rhythm*. Vera had begun the role of Maria in *For Whom the Bell Tolls*, but after the first week of filming, she was replaced by Ingrid Bergman.

A very rare leg-art photo of LORETTA YOUNG, taken in 1952, when she played a magician's assistant opposite Jeff Chandler in Universal's *Because of You.*

This pose of JANE WYMAN is from Columbia's *Let's Do It Again.* Jane won an Oscar for *Johnny Belinda.* She is the former wife of President Ronald Reagan.

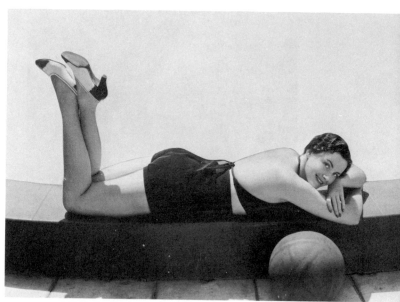

FRIEDA INESCORT was a publicist before she turned to stage acting and finally reached films in 1935.

A truly rare leg-art shot of GREER GARSON, who was playing a showgirl in the 1948 movie *Julie Misbehaves.* An Oscar winner for *Mrs. Miniver,* Greer now lives with her husband, Buddy Fogelson, in Santa Fe, New Mexico.

133

The great child singing star of many popular MGM musicals KATHRYN GRAYSON sings today in supper clubs and on the concert stage.

A Paramount child star, MITZI GREEN played the title role in *Little Orphan Annie* and portrayed Becky Thatcher to Jackie Coogan's *Tom Sawyer*. She was still in her teens when she left films, but she returned briefly in 1952 to appear in an Abbott and Costello comedy. At her death in 1969 at the age of forty-eight, she was married to director Joseph Pevney.

A 1935 Oscar nominee at the age of thirteen for *These Three*, BONITA GRANVILLE appeared in fifty-five films before her retirement in 1949. Today she and her husband, producer Jack Wrather, turn out *Lassie* films. They live in Palm Springs.

VIRGINIA GREY, a longtime girlfriend of Clark Gable, appeared with him in MGM's *Idiot's Delight*. Today film producer Ross Hunter calls her his good-luck charm and casts her in his movies whenever possible.

Doris Hill came into films in 1927, left the screen in 1934, and now makes her home near Phoenix, Arizona.

In films since 1931, Karen Morley became a victim of the notorious Hollywood blacklist and appeared in no more films after the 1952 production of *M*. Now in her seventies, she acted recently in the short-lived TV series *Banyon*.

Another rare leg-art pose, from Miriam Hopkins, a star who generally managed to avoid such photos. An Oscar nominee for *Becky Sharpe*, the great Paramount star of the thirties died in 1972.

A British musical star, Jessie Matthews was known as "the lady with the loveliest legs in London." Today she is an attractive grandmother.

The film was Paramount's *Evenings for Sale*, and SARI MARITZA's leading man was Herbert Marshall, sophisticated male movie star.

JEANETTE MAC DONALD was a popular singing star for twenty years. Her leading men included such stalwarts as Nelson Eddy, Maurice Chevalier, Ramon Novarro, Allan Jones, Robert Young, and her husband, Gene Raymond.

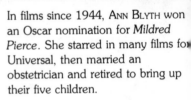

In films since 1944, ANN BLYTH won an Oscar nomination for *Mildred Pierce*. She starred in many films for Universal, then married an obstetrician and retired to bring up their five children.

Joan's kid sister GLORIA BLONDELL was under contract to Columbia at the time, but her acting career failed to rise above supporting roles.

136

Twice nominated for Oscars, ELSA LANCHESTER, wife of Charles Laughton, also had a career on the stage. She is here seen singing *The Dame, Melinda Mame* while starring in a revue, *High Time,* with the Yale Puppeteers.

JULIE BISHOP began her career in 1923 at the age of nine in *Maytime,* under the name Jacqueline Wells. Warners gave her a new name in 1941, and she made seventy-four movies. Here, she's publicizing her role opposite Humphrey Bogart in *Action in the North Atlantic.*

MARY BRIAN called herself a perpetual ingenue. Her screen debut was in the 1924 version of *Peter Pan,* and her last screen appearance was in 1948 in *The Dragnet.* After retiring, she became a very successful portrait artist.

FRANCES FARMER, a talented actress highly praised for her performance in *Come and Get It*, ran into troubled times, spent seven years in a mental hospital, and failed in a comeback try. She died in 1970 at fifty-six.

GLENDA FARRELL specialized in portraying wisecracking blonds, notably in her *Torchy Blane* movies for Warners. Just before her death in 1971 she had been on stage as Julie Harris's mother in *Forty Carats*.

An important star of the early twenties MADGE BELLAMY had successfully bridged the gap between the silents and the talkies.

SALLY EILERS arrived in the movies the same year that sound did. Once married to western star Hoot Gibson, she had three subsequent husbands— producer Harry Joe Brown, navy captain Howard Barney, and director John Morse.

138

In films since the late twenties, Loretta Young's sister SALLY BLANE married actor-director Norman Foster in 1934 and retired from the screen five years later after *Charlie Chan at Treasure Island.*

Ernest A. Ba

DEANNA DURBIN, a child singing star who reportedly saved a major studio, Universal, from going broke. Today she lives in retirement in a village fifty miles from Paris.

A true beauty with a superb figure, ROSEMARY DE CAMP has been in films since 1941.

FRANCES DRAKE was in movies during the mid-thirties. She retired following her marriage to the son of England's Earl of Suffolk. She is here publicizing her role as a Spanish dancer opposite George Raft in Paramount's *The Trumpet Blows*.

JULIETTE COMPTON as she appeared in *Berkeley Square*.

LITA CHEVRET striking a leg-art pose to help publicize her role in Radio Pictures' musical comedy *The Cuckoo*.

MARY CARLISLE entered movies in 1922 at the age of ten and later played leading roles in dozens of films. She retired in 1943 after *Dead Men Walk* and later became the manager of a posh Beverly Hills beauty salon. This photo is from MGM's *Safety First*.

CLAUDETTE COLBERT showed that she was an accomplished dramatic actress and a skilled comedienne, and she did wonders for leg art when she hitched up her skirt to beg a ride in *It Happened One Night*. Now in her seventies Colbert spends most of her time at her home in Barbados and keeps apartments in Paris and New York for occasional brief visits.

KATHRYN CRAWFORD helping to publicize the MGM movie *Flying High*.

NANCY CARROLL began making films in the late twenties and went on to become one of Paramount's brightest stars. She was nominated for an Oscar for *The Devil's Holiday*. At the time of her death in 1965, she was fifty-eight.

The shapely songstress GERTRUDE NIESEN was starring at Los Angeles' Greek Theater in the 1948 production of *Anything Goes* when she struck this leg-art pose.

GERALDINE FITZGERALD, as the third in a romantic triangle including George Sanders and Ella Raines, in Universal's *Uncle Harry*.

MARTHA RAYE exploited her generous mouth to achieve stardom as a comedienne, but the Raye limbs were also among the loveliest of her era. Here she's plugging her role with Bob Hope in Paramount's *Never Say Die*.

RUTH ROMAN was a popular star of the forties and fifties. She is still active, often appearing in TV character roles.

MOZELLE BRITTON was a dancer who struck this provocative pose while appearing in films at Columbia.

GINGER ROGERS began in films in 1930 at the age of nineteen. This is a delectable leg-art pose from early in her career.

KATHLEEN BURKE became the Panther Woman when the nineteen-year-old Chicago beauty bested sixty thousand aspirants to gain the role in Paramount's *Island of Lost Souls.*

GLORIA DE HAVEN had a great body and knew how to display it.

During a twenty-two-year screen career, ESTHER RALSTON appeared in more than 150 films. Here she models a negligee for her role with Lawrence Tibbett in MGM's *The Southerner.*

143

In 1939, VEDA ANN BORG's face was completely reconstructed by plastic surgery following a terrible automobile accident. Veda, who often played tough character roles, died in 1973 at the age of fifty-eight.

BINNIE BARNES came into the movies in 1931, married producer Mike Frankovich in 1940, and now divides her time among three children, three grandchildren, and an occasional return to films, such as in *Forty Carats*.

A leg art photo of the great dramatic star BETTE DAVIS who shunned such poses. Bette won Oscars for both *Dangerous* and *Jezebel*.

A rare leg-art pose by the lovely DONNA REED who won an Academy Award as best supporting actress for her work in *From Here to Eternity*. Donna retired after her third marriage in 1974 to United States Army Colonel Grover Asmus.

A very early leg-art pose by the famous German actress LIL DAGOVER who entered films in 1919. Maximilian Schell lured her from a thirty-five-year retirement in 1974 to play a role in *The Pedestrian*.

When this picture of CLAUDIA DELL was taken, Tom Mix was embarking on his first talking picture, *Destry Rides Again*, with Claudia as his leading lady.

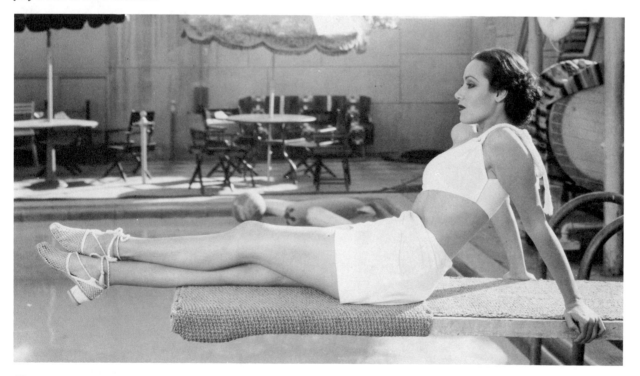

Glamorous Mexican film star DOLORES DEL RIO strikes a fetching leg-art pose in 1935. Today, in her seventies, she is still a dazzling beauty.

The attractive Metropolitan Opera
soprano MARGUERITE PIAZZA relaxes
poolside while in Hollywood on a
1951 vacation.

NADINE DORE in a 1932 leg-art
pose that epitomizes the classic
stance of the skirt lift.

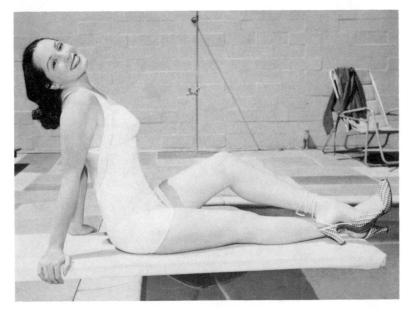

GLORIA GRAHAME, modeling a 1952 swimsuit
style while appearing at MGM as Dick
Powell's wife in *Tribute to a Bad Man*.

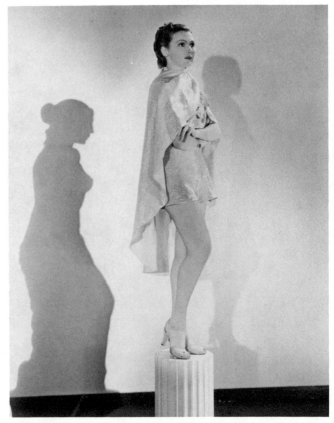

A blond star of the thirties and forties,
ASTRID ALLWYN, is shown here vying with
Venus, the goddess of love and beauty.

SHELLEY WINTERS in a leg-art pose while playing a featured role in Paramount's 1949 version of *The Great Gatsby*.

KATHARINE HEPBURN shunned leg art unless a role demanded it—as in her stage performance for *As You Like It* at the Biltmore Theatre in Los Angeles.

JUDY HOLLIDAY specialized on the screen as a dumb blond in such hits as *Born Yesterday* and *The Solid Gold Cadillac*.

JUNE HAVER appeared prominently in such films as *Home in Indiana, The Dolly Sisters,* and *I'll Get By.* She's been Fred MacMurray's wife for more than twenty years, and the mother of twin daughters.

Norway's pretty Olympic figure-skating champion SONJA HENIE went on to become a great star in 20th Century-Fox ice-skating musicals.

Not only did MGM's dancing star ELEANOR POWELL have gorgeous legs, but she possessed a set of the most talented gams ever in films.

A famous leg-art photo of AVA GARDNER

MAGDA GABOR, another of the beauteous Gabor sisters, was not as famous as Zsa Zsa and Eva, but she knew how to kick up her heels for a cameraman.

ALLISON HAYES was featured prominently in *Francis Joins the WACs* and *Sign of the Pagan*. She is striking a leg art pose to publicize her role in *The Hypnotic Eye.*

EVA GABOR was the first of the Gabor trio to break into the movies. She's still very much in view.

150

Hungarian actress ZSA ZSA GABOR has epitomized glamour and sophistication since she began making films in 1952. She's always had a lot of fans and she's had a lot of husbands too. The costume she's wearing is for her role in *Moulin Rouge.*

Someone once said about ESTHER WILLIAMS "Wet she's an actress; dry she's not." Her swimusicals for MGM were smashing successes, and she was a top box-office star. She is posing prettily for *Dangerous When Wet*.

Pretty blond leading lady HELEN WALKER made her debut opposite Alan Ladd in *Lucky Jordan*, but illness forced her retirement in 1955, and death claimed her at the age of forty-seven in 1968.

Only seven years old when she made her movie bow in *A Midsummer Night's Dream*, HELEN WESTCOTT is here older and considerably more seductive.

RITA JOHNSON was an MGM actress who invariably played bitchy roles. She died in 1965 at age fifty-two. She is shown here in the Columbia film *Here Comes Mr. Jordan*.

ARLENE WHELAN, manicurist who was discovered by director H. Bruce "Lucky" Humberstone in a Hollywood Boulevard barbershop was whisked to screen fame. Here she is while playing the other woman in Paramount's *Dear Wife*.

151

DEBRA PAGET is shown in a scene from Columbia's *Most Dangerous Man Alive*. Now married to wealthy Chinese oilman Louis Kung, she lives in Houston.

JANE POWELL was a musical star who came into films as a teenager during the forties. She recently staged a comeback, replacing Debbie Reynolds on the Broadway stage in the musical *Irene*.

Warner Bros. actress MARTHA VICKERS's best role was as the retarded heiress in the film *The Big Sleep*. Once wed to Mickey Rooney, Martha died in 1971 at the age of forty-six.

LUANA PATTEN had two careers at Walt Disney Studios—as a child star and later as a leading lady. Here she poses in the inevitable wicker chair (every studio portrait gallery had at least one) while appearing in MGM's *Home from the Hill*.

A direct descendant of a famous early California family, ELENA VERDUGO became a star in both movies and TV. Here she adds glamour to her role as Gene Autry's leading lady in Columbia's *The Big Sombrero*.

AMELITA VARGAS dancing a sultry samba in a nightclub sequence for the Pat O'Brien production *Perilous Holiday.*

A World War II pinup poster of SHIRLEY JONES doing her bit for Uncle Sam's navy. Shirley won an Oscar for her supporting role in *Elmer Gantry.*

Ample-bosomed JAYNE MANSFIELD was touted as a successor to Marilyn Monroe, and she pulled out all stops to qualify. However, an auto accident claimed her life when she was thirty-four.

153

154   The exotic dancing star LILI ST. CYR was recognized among her peers as the most accomplished ecdysiast of them all. She appeared in such films as *Son of Sinbad* and *The Naked and the Dead* but with less display of flesh than in her headlining nightclub act.

A 1934 Wampus Baby Star, GERTRUDE MICHAEL had played Calpurnia in C. B. De Mille's *Cleopatra* and also starred in a series of *Sophie Lang* movies.

Well-known for her brassy-blond roles, MARION MARTIN actually came from a Philadelphia Main Line family and was educated at private schools in Europe.

The busty blond JOI LANSING was seen on screen in such films as *A Hole in the Head* and *Who Was That Lady?* and on TV with Bob Cummings in his popular comedy series.

The famous MGM dancing star ANN MILLER poses for classic Fourth of July cheesecake. Her 1972 autobiography was appropriately titled *Miller's High Life*.

In films since 1924, LEILA HYAMS retired after her marriage to top Hollywood agent Phil Berg. Here she is shown posing prettily at Malibu Beach during her contract days at MGM.

MARILYN MAXWELL was Kirk Douglas's love in *Champion* and later performed as a female foil for such comedy stars as Bob Hope in *The Lemon Drop Kid* and Jerry Lewis in *Rock-a-bye Baby*. She entertained GIs all over the globe in both World War II and the Korean conflict. She died in 1972 at age forty-nine.

A Universal contract player, GRACE MC DONALD was featured in the comedy musical *Cross Your Fingers*.

CONSTANCE MOORE began in films in the late thirties, enjoyed a very successful career as a singer and actress, and now lives happily in Beverly Hills, a contented grandmother.

RITA MORENO, a talented Latin singer-dancer-actress, won an Academy Award as best supporting actress for her performance in the classic hit *West Side Story*.

157

VERA MILES came into the movies in 1952 as a glamour star and is still on the screen demonstrating her fine dramatic talents in character roles.

Few actress-singers' careers can approach the success and longevity of LENA HORNE's headlining life on stage and in films.

JUNE HAVOC appeared in silent films as a child actress in Hal Roach comedies but began her adult acting career later. She's the sister of Gypsy Rose Lee.

158

DOLORES GRAY, a popular musical star, played the title role in *Annie Get Your Gun* in London, won a Tony on Broadway, and made her movie debut in MGM's *It's Always Fair Weather*.

MARSHA HUNT refused to pose in a bathing suit until she was handed a role in *College Holiday*, in which she gives Leif Erikson an underwater on-screen kiss.

In films since the late twenties DOROTHY GRANGER used to appear on screen as Leon Errol's wife in two-reelers.

RMEN MIRANDA was a 20th Century-Fox musical of the forties known as the Brazilian mbshell. She popularized Latin tempos and es—and platform slippers for women. rmen died in 1955 at age forty-one.

PIPER LAURIE's real name was Rosetta Jacobs. The Fourth of July meant reporting to the Universal portrait gallery for poses like this one.

Many times a nominee for an Academy Award, DEBORAH KERR was hardly ever caught in a leg-art pose. Here, she is taking a call on a Columbia stage during the filming of *From Here to Eternity.*

ANDREA LEEDS, in a bathing-fashion pose spotlighting her role in Universal's *Youth Takes a Fling.*

160

VERA HRUBA RALSTON began her screen career as an ice-skating queen and made twenty-six movies for Republic. Her late husband, Herbert I. Yates, was Republic's bossman.

BETTY HUTTON, the celebrated comedienne, is shown here in a comic pose to promote *Here Come the Waves*. No one will ever forget her rousing film performance as the title star of MGM's *Annie Get Your Gun*.

ABBE LANE, once married to bandleader Xavier Cugat and lead femme vocalist for his orchestra, strikes a leggy pose to publicize her dramatic role in Columbia's *Chicago Syndicate*.

161

GLORIA STUART came to the screen shortly after sound arrived, and she retired from films in 1946.

ROSELLA TOWNE was snapped at the Warner Bros. movie lot during filming of *The Brooklyn Cowboy*.

PAULETTE GODDARD was once nominated for an Oscar for her performance in *So Proudly We Hail*. She is now retired and living in Switzerland.

162

Only SUSAN HAYWARD's superb talents as a dramatic actress overshadowed the dazzling certainty that her figure was among the best in the cinema world.

EVELYN KEYES posed for a swinging leg-art scene prior to starting her role with Larry Parks in Columbia's *The Jolson Story*.

A reigning screen star for many years, MERLE OBERON won an Oscar nomination for *The Dark Angel*. In 1975 she married her fourth husband, Robert Wolders, fifteen years her junior. They were active in Hollywood society circles. She died in 1979.

The great musical star of Broadway and Hollywood MARY MARTIN shows off a pair of the prettiest legs in show business. She recently penned her autobiography, *My Heart Belongs*. She makes her home in Palm Springs.

DIXIE DUNBAR, a dancing 20th Century-Fox stock actress, hoofed her final scene in *Alexander's Ragtime Band*. Years later she was an anonymous dancing star on television as the unseen girl inside an oversized pack of Old Gold cigarettes.

After many roles in period pictures, ANGELA LANSBURY revealed her gorgeous limbs in the Can Can number she did for MGM's *The Harvey Girls*.

Ex-wife of the late Bruce Cabot, ADRIENNE AMES specialized in society-girl screen roles. Judging from this leg-art photo, she probably introduced the fashion of high-heeled shoes for swimming.

A professional dancer, YVONNE DE CARLO (real name, Peggy Middleton) won a nationwide contest to play the title role in Universal's *Salome: Where She Danced*.

MARGUERITE CHURCHILL was once married to male star George O'Brien. She came into films in 1929, has long since retired, and lives in Portugal.

Beautiful JEANNE CRAIN was also an accomplished actress, as attested by her Academy Award nomination for *Pinky*.

A popular RKO leading lady, JUNE CLYDE is shown here demonstrating the healthful advantage of a sunbath under cellophane—and plugging her role in *The Cohens and Kellys in Hollywood*. She retired in 1934 and moved to England with her film-director husband, Thornton Freeland.

The first of the beauties to be selected for MGM's *Zie Girl*, GEORGIA CARROLL slipped into this Adrian-designe costume to play the Goddess of Dawn in the "You Stepped Out of a Dream" musical number.

SUSANNA FOSTER appeared prominently in many film musicals of the forties, but today she devotes her energies to a career on Wall Street.

At the age of seven NANETTE FABRAY was one of the *Our Gang* kids on the screen. As an adult, she became a Broadway musical-comedy star, then soared to TV prominence for her comedy work opposite Sid Caesar.

A young RKO star of the 40s, MYRNA DELL was often a romantic item with Howard Hughes. Today Myrna runs a party-planning business in Hollywood.

JOAN FULTON adds a sexy look to a movie western as she plays a saloon entertainer in *The Vigilantes Return.*

When she reached stardom at 20th Century-Fox, LINDA DARNELL was still a teenager, and a man required the personal permission of Darryl F. Zanuck, studio chief, to take her on a date. She was forty-three in 1965 when death claimed her.

JANE FRAZEE, a leading actress in many cheapie musicals of the forties, bowed out of films in the mid-fifties and now sells real estate in Newport Beach, California. She's shown here while appearing in Columbia's *Hello Mom*.

A fashion pose of desert toggery during VIRGINIA FIELD's days as a 20th Century-Fox contractee.

SIDNEY FOX's name sounded masculine, but she was thoroughly female. In *Bad Sister* she played the title role, billed over Bette Davis. She was only thirty-one at the time of her death in 1942.

An onscreen leading lady in 1948, ANNE FRANCIS played prominent roles in such films as *A Lion Is in the Streets*, *Bad Day at Black Rock*, *The Blackboard Jungle*, and *Funny Girl*.

JINX FALKENBURG was a tournament-class tennis player as well as a screen beauty. Here she demonstrates how she introduced the Bambalero in Columbia's *The Gay Señorita*.

RHONDA FLEMING had one of the best figures of all time and didn't avoid showing it, as she does here in her role as a harem beauty in Universal-International's *Yankee Pasha.*

BETTA ST. JOHN, a recruit from Broadway, where she had scored a hit as the native girl in *South Pacific*, made her screen debut with Cary Grant and Deborah Kerr in *Dream Wife.*

A screen beauty of the mid-fifties and sixties, BARBARA NICHOLS had the kind of figure that leg-art photographers dreamed of.

172

ALICE FAYE in the custom hosiery the studios often hired a Hollywood hosiery manufacturer (Willys of Hollywood) to fashion for leg-art photography.

SIMONE SIMON made her Hollywood film bow as the star of 20th Century-Fox's *Girls' Dormitory,* in which Tyrone Power played a brief bit part. Later, she made headlines in a sexy Hollywood scandal. She eventually returned to Paris and, as late as 1973, was still appearing in French films.

EVA MARIE SAINT is shown here in a leggy pose on location in Yosemite National Park for *36 Hours.* Eva won an Oscar for her very first film, *On the Waterfront.* She now puts her considerable talent to work in character roles.

173

ALEXIS SMITH as she appeared in the western *South of St. Louis*, with Joel McCrea and Zachary Scott. Married to Craig Stevens, she left the screen more than fifteen years ago, then resurfaced as a Broadway star of musicals and drama.

A rare leg-art pose by GALE SONDERGAARD, one of the screen's finest dramatic actresses and winner of the first supporting-actress Oscar in 1936 for *Anthony Adverse.* In 1976 she made a heralded screen comeback in the top supporting role for *The Return of a Man Called Horse,* starring Richard Harris. This 1930s-style pose is in connection with Paramount's *Never Say Die.*

A rare leg-art photo of the great actress and comedienne ROSALIND RUSSELL who never considered her figure appropriate for pinups. The outfit is a movie costume worn for a rowing scene in Columbia's *A Woman of Distinction.*

A beautiful blond from the Deep South, ANN SAVAGE leaves no doubt that she's calling attention to Halloween in this leg-art picture. She was under contract to Columbia at the time, making her debut in *One Dangerous Night* with Warren William.

DEBBIE REYNOLDS, now going strong as a big-time supper-club headliner, spent many years at MGM. This skyrocket pose honoring the Fourth of July looks like the product of a retoucher's ingenuity.

A feminine star of the forties, ELLA RAINES left films following her marriage to Brigadier General Robin Olds, former commandant of the Air Force academy. This leg-art photo was snapped in 1944 at RKO.

DOROTHY BURGESS had been Warner Baxter's leading lady in the screen classic *In Old Arizona,* but lasting movie stardom eluded her. She died at age fifty-four in 1961.

GERALDINE PAGE was a three-time Academy Award nominee for *Hondo, Summer and Smoke,* and *Sweet Bird of Youth.* This photograph, taken in 1961, is from *Sweet Bird of Youth,* in which she starred with Paul Newman.

From the age of sixteen until she was twenty-
five, FAITH DOMERGUE was under personal contract
to Howard Hughes. A few years ago it was
announced that she was going to write a book
called *My Life With Howard Hughes*, but it never
materialized.

WENDY BARRIE invaded Hollywood and hit stardom in the
thirties, but the movie town eventually shunned her
because of her association with mobster Bugsy Siegel. She
went East and became a top radio star, but when last
heard of she was semi-invalid in an Eastern nursing home.
This photo is vintage 1935.

A rare leg-art pose of the great star INGRID
BERGMAN, who usually shunned pinup
photographs. Ingrid won best-actress
Oscars for *Gaslight* and *Anastasia* and a
supporting-actress Academy Award for
Murder on the Orient Express.

ELINOR DONAHUE came to films in the mid-forties as a teenager. After her marriage to producer Harry Ackerman, she played only a few screen roles.

As a child VANESSA BROWN was one of the original *Quiz Kids* of radio fame. After her marriage to director Mark Sandrich, she turned to a career as a writer of novels, nonfiction, newspaper articles, and TV scripts.

DORIS DAY, as she appeared in an imagination sequence for MGM's *The Glass Bottom Boat.*

179

MARI BLANCHARD starred in many Universal westerns of the fifties, plus an occasional sex-and-sand drama. She was forty-three at the time of her death in 1970.

MB-8

After appearing in *The Girl from Havana* in 1940, the Hungarian-born actress STEFFI DUNA married the film's leading man, Dennis O'Keefe, and retired to devote her full time to being a housewife until O'Keefe's death in 1968. She now sells Beverly Hills real estate.

GALE STORM came to the movies in 1939 as winner of the Jesse L. Lasky Gateway to Hollywood talent search featured on Lasky's radio show. She appeared prominently in a great many movies, achieved stardom on TV in *My Little Margie*, and today is looking for a new TV series to continue her career. In private life, she's the wife of Lee Bonnell, who won the male competition in Lasky's talent search.

LESLIE BROOKS, under contract to Columbia in the forties, played supporting roles. Her last film was *Blonde Ice* in 1948. She is now married to a prominent West Coast real estate developer and mother of three grown daughters.

ROSALIE ROY.

184

LARAINE DAY, once the wife of Leo "Lippy" Durocher, has been in films since the late thirties. More recently, she played a role in *Medical Center* at MGM, the same lot where she had appeared in seven episodes of another hit MGM-TV medical series, *Dr. Kildare*.

DOROTHY MALONE won an Oscar for her role in *Written on the Wind*. She is shown here in a 1945 leg-art pose. After four years on TV's *Peyton Place*, she quit films and moved to Dallas. She continues to appear in stage plays and occasionally flies back to Hollywood for a movie or TV performance.

VERA-ELLEN, a vivacious dancing star of the screen, is shown here in association with her co-starring role with Fred Astaire in MGM's *The Belle of New York*. She retired from the screen in 1959.

SANDRA DEE was seventeen when she struck this pose in the Warner Bros. portrait gallery, sometimes affectionately known as Gallery Beach. The movie was *A Summer Place*.

VIRGINIA DALE, an accomplished comedienne, is seen here in her featured role for Paramount's *Las Vegas Nights*.

This is leg art plus one, a composite photo in which JEFF DONNELL demonstrates a physical-fitness routine and also plugs her role in Columbia's *What's Buzzin', Cousin?*

BARBARA BATES, best remembered from the final scene of *All About Eve,* is shown in a leg-art pose promoting her role as Mickey Rooney's girl in Columbia's *All Ashore.* She was forty-three at the time of her death in 1969.

POLLY BERGEN entered films in 1950, enjoyed fine success on the screen, and is now the wealthy manufacturer of a beauty lotion.

ANNE BANCROFT, who won an Oscar for *The Miracle Worker.* Anne is married to comedy producer Mel Brooks.

JUDITH BARRETT, seen reminding everyone that Easter is just around the corner. Judith played the other woman in the Bob Hope-Bing Crosby-Dorothy Lamour starrer *Road to Singapore*.

ROSEMARIE BOWE entered films during the fifties and signed to a Columbia contract after appearing on a *Life* cover. She's better known today as Mrs. Robert Stack.

GRACE BRADLEY was married for thirty-five years to the late William "Hopalong Cassidy" Boyd and makes her home in Newport Beach, California.

VALERIE BETTIS, like all female dancers, knew how to keep in shape and how to show that shape. Here she is as she appeared in Columbia's *Love Song*.

JEAN PETERS found overnight fame opposite Tyrone Power in 1947's *The Captain from Castille* and played star roles in eighteen subsequent movies. After she married billionaire Howard Hughes in 1957, she not only retired, but literally disappeared from sight, rarely appearing publicly. After their divorce she married film producer Stanley Hough. Friends say she will never reveal details of her marriage to Hughes.

This is the leg-art photo that went to newspapers on the hottest day of the year. YVONNE CRAIG, a delectable teenager, came to films in 1960 and appeared in such movies as *Gidget* and *Quick Before It Melts,* the latter explaining this pose.

, an Olympic ice-skating champion, also starred on s in Ice Capades. She was a dramatic actress and a ina. Retired in 1954, she makes her home in m, on the outskirts of London. This photo is from gram's *Suspense.*

Among Jo Ann Pflug's films in the seventies were *M*A*S*H, Catlow,* and *Where Does It Hurt?*

The curvaceous singer Connie Russell made her movie bow in Columbia's *Cruisin' Down the River.* After a few subsequent movie roles she took her headline act back to the supper-club circuit.

The desert is a backdrop in a studio portrait gallery, but there's nothing phony about the classic lines of Marjorie Riordan, who brightened the screen with her performance in *Stage Door Canteen.*

first movie, *The Outlaw,* was two years from filming to
se, but in between, Jane Russell became a star as a
t of publicity heaped upon her. Her discoverer was
ard Hughes, and during Jane's entire film career she was
by the Hughes Tool Co. Today she does bra
mercials on TV and appears occasionally in dinner
ters.

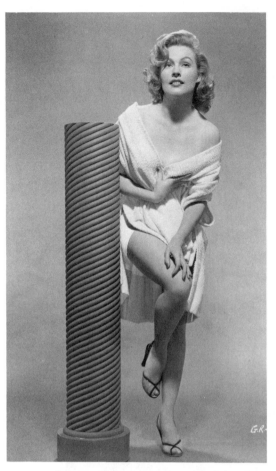

A singer on screen and in nightclubs, GALE ROBBINS played a theatrical star in *Calamity Jane,* a Doris Day–Howard Keel starrer for Warner Bros.

LORI NELSON's career began in comedy series at Universal such as the Francis the Mule films with Donald O'Connor and the Ma and Pa Kettle homespun howlers starring Marjorie Main and Percy Kilbride. Lori was once married to Johnny Mann of the Johnny Mann singers.

196

lumbia movie boss Harry Cohn made KIM NOVAK a star.
ne of the best examples that Cohn knew his business
s Kim's eventual performance co-starring with Frank
natra and Rita Hayworth in *Pal Joey*. Today Kim lives in
house overlooking the Pacific at Big Sur.

A rare leg-art pose by BARBARA RUSH, who rarely got involved in what was known as holiday art. Recruited from the Pasadena Playhouse, Barbara starred in many Universal films with such leading men as Rock Hudson and Tony Curtis.

A Conover model, ELAINE STEWART was signed by MGM, made her film bow in *Sailor Beware,* and was promptly dubbed Star of Tomorrow. MGM also publicized her as the most beautiful girl in pictures.

DINAH SHORE was a great singing star and leading lady of the screen but never achieved the fame she enjoys today as a TV talk-show hostess. This leg-art pose is no sham.

JAN STERLING played Humphrey Bogart's wife in Columbia's boxing drama *The Harder They Fall.*

199

The daughter of actress Anna Lee, VENETIA STEVENSON was once married to Russ Tamblyn and also to Don Everly of the Everly Brothers. She is now retired from the screen.

LOUISE FRANKLIN as she appeared in the role of a harem beauty in MGM's *Kismet*.

JILL ST. JOHN still has one of the most seductive figures ever to grace a movie screen. Moviegoers were once almost treated to the St. John body sans clothing in the James Bond movie *Diamonds Are Forever*. Today she lives grandly in Aspen, Colorado, and accepts few of the film offers that come her way.

CYD CHARISSE—One of the great dancing stars of the entertainment world, Cyd, a Texan from Amarillo, struck this pose during filming of MGM's "The Band Wagon." Today she heads a top night club act with her singer-husband Tony Martin.

202

A Parisian dancer with the Ballet des Champs-Élysées before MGM signed her in 1950 to star with Gene Kelly in *An American in Paris*, LESLIE CARON has been twice nominated for Oscars, for her performances in *Lili* and *The L-Shaped Room*.

Under contract to Universal, PEGGIE CASTLE played many feminine leads. She died at age forty-five in 1973.

204

When Columbia sought the perfect female actress for the title role in *The Pretty Girl*, the search ended with JOAN CAULFIELD. She devotes her time today to stock-company appearances on stages in Texas, Florida, and the Midwest.

JANIS CARTER enjoying a day of Pacific sailing while posing
for the publicity camera to help promote her role with
Franchot Tone and Janet Blair in *I Love Trouble*.

A singer and an actress, KITTY CARLISLE appeared in films during the thirties. One of her roles was with the Marx Brothers in *A Night at the Opera*.

ROSEMARY CLOONEY, a hit recording star and a popular screen actress, married José Ferrer and retired to become the mother of five children. They are now divorced.

Here's a rare photo of ABIGAIL ADAMS, a bathing beauty who dares go near the water. Abigail was appearing in Columbia's *Mary Lou* at the time she enjoyed this frolic at a nearby Pacific beach.

JULIE ADAMS played mostly dramatic roles at Universal, but when the studio publicists got a look at those gorgeous gams, they slapped on insurance for a million dollars and sent the Adams leg-art poses all over the world. She is shown here in a delicious slice of Christmas cheesecake.

A movie doll of the thirties, JUDITH ALLEN appeared in such films as *Bright Eyes, Boots and Saddles,* and *Port of Missing Girls.*

ELLEN DREW came into movies in the thirties, appeared in such films as *Sing You Sinners, My Favorite Spy, Johnny O'Clock,* and *Stars in My Crown.* Today she lives quietly at her desert home near Palm Springs.

It's easy to see why DENISE DARCEL had no problem winning a big role in the Esther Williams starrer *Dangerous When Wet* for MGM. Now the wife of a wealthy health-spa owner, she lives in retirement in Florida and occasionally acts in dinner theaters and TV commercials.

A statuesque redhead, ARLENE DAHL was a popular film star of the fifties. Today she's a highly successful businesswoman in New York, merchandising cosmetics.

Britain's contender for the sexpot crown sought by Monroe, Bardot, and others, DIANA DORS is shown ring the promotion bells for two RKO movies, *I Married a Woman* and *The Unholy Wife*.

LTP-ADV-14

PATRICIA ELLIS, a Warners leading lady of the thirties, rang up forty-two film roles during an eight-year career. She was fifty-four at the time of her death in 1970. Shown here with Venus, she was publicizing her role in Columbia's *Venus Makes Trouble.*

Once married to Sammy Davis, Jr., MAY BRITT was a leading lady of the fifties in such movies as *The Young Lions, The Blue Angel,* and *Secrets of a Woman.*

TA EKBERG, representing her native Sweden in the Miss
verse beauty contest in the early fifties. Anita was a
list and winner of a Universal movie contract. Here she
ws her winning points in a pose outside the
ionable Hollywood restaurant Don the
chcomber's.

Formerly married to Steve McQueen, NEILE ADAMS was a dancer and actress who enjoyed a steady if not star-studded screen career.

A former cover girl, DUSTY ANDERSON graced the screen in many Columbia movies of the forties. She is seen here heralding Halloween with typical holiday leg art. Dusty now lives on the island of Majorca and devotes most of her time to painting.

CONSTANCE TOWERS, singer, actress, and wife of actor John Gavin, appeared in movies of the fifties and sixties. She now devotes her career to roles in civic light opera and musical comedy.

NANCY KWAN, Hong Kong's gorgeous gift to Hollywood, first burst onto the American screen as William Holden's object of desire in the movie *The World of Suzie Wong.* Next, Ross Hunter starred her in *Flower Drum Song,* with spectacular success.

AQUANETTA, the sultry Cheyenne Indian beauty, specialized in sexy-native-girl portrayals of the forties in such movies as *Jungle Woman* and *Tarzan and the Leopard Woman.* Today she lives in Scottsdale, Arizona where she hosts a TV talk show.

The attractive Italian actress LILIANE MONTEVECCHI puts dramatic punch into leg art.

A former Broadway dancer before she went on to become one of the biggest TV stars of prime time, MARY TYLER MOORE shows that her gams are as delectable as they are talented. She was formerly married to TV executive Grant Tinker.

216

Italian leg art had a look of its own, as demonstrated here by one of Rome's sexiest movie queens, ELSA MARTINELLI.

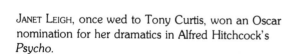

JANET LEIGH, once wed to Tony Curtis, won an Oscar nomination for her dramatics in Alfred Hitchcock's *Psycho*.

217

Death claimed KAY KENDALL, the lovely British comedienne and wife of Rex Harrison, in 1959 at the age of thirty-three. Among movie fans she lives on in such films as *Les Girls*, *Doctor in the House*, and *The Reluctant Debutante*.

BARBARA LAWRENCE was appearing in MGM's *Twelve Angry Men* at the time she struck this fetching leg-art pose. The photo caption labeled her "outdorable," but Barbara was actually in the Gallery Beach section of MGM's portrait studio.

An Oscar nominee for *Peyton Place,* HOPE LANGE is also a leading leg-art lady.

Movita, shown here as a dancehall doll in Columbia's *Apache Ambush*. Movita was once married to Marlon Brando.

An Oscar nominee for *The Bachelor Party*, Carolyn Jones is shown here as she appeared in Warner's *Marjorie Morningstar*. In 1976 she announced her return to the screen after seven years as a novelist.

This leg-art pose of SHIRLEY MACLAINE was taken during the filming of the MGM release *Some Came Running.*

SHIRLEY MACLAINE was proud of her pony days as a Broadway chorine, and she's again on stage, dancing as one of the headliners of the supper-club circuit.

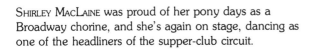

221

The men in TERRY MOORE's life included football star Glenn Davis, millionaire Stuart Cramer III, actor Glenn Ford, statesman Henry Kissinger—and Howard Hughes, to whom Terry says she was once secretly wed.

BETSY PALMER is shown striking a sexy pose in the Columbia portrait gallery for her role in *The Other Life of Lynn Stuart*.

The fabulously proportioned JULIE NEWMAR was billed as Julie Newmeyer when she danced in MGM's *Seven Brides for Seven Brothers*.

MAMIE VAN DOREN was named by Universal after a president's wife and a big winner on TV's *$64,000 Question*. She was actually Joan Olander from Rowena, South Dakota.

MILLY VITALE decorated the movie screen in such films as *The Seven Little Foys*, *War and Peace*, and *A Breath of Scandal*.

During summer hot spells, movie press agents loved to rush to the newspapers with cooling leg art. EDY WILLIAMS, who never minded showing what she had, appeared in Ross Hunter's *The Pad (And How to Use It)*.

NATALIE WOOD seen showing off the Schizophrenic Wardrobe designed by Edith Head for Wood's role in the MGM comedy *Penelope*.

After a career of fifteen years and seventy pictures, JOAN WOODBURY left the movies to produce and direct plays, operas, and musicals for community theaters in Redlands, California, and Palm Springs.

225

The celebrated dancing star GWEN VERDON in her costume for her leading role in *Damn Yankees.*

A star of the forties and fifties, ADELE JERGENS appeared in many Columbia sex-and-sand movies. Long and happily married to actor Glenn Langan, she makes her home in San Fernando Valley.

A shot of the lovely actress JOANNE WOODWARD, known in private life as Mrs. Paul Newman.

MARTHA HYER married the noted film producer Hal Wallis in 1966 and gave up her acting career four years later to be free to accompany her husband on his world travels.

BARBARA HALE was here playing a nightclub singer and girlfriend of a mobster in the Sam Katzman movie *The Houston Story* for Columbia.

JUNE HAVER struck this leg-art pose shortly after the end of World War II to call attention to a Lloyds of London insurance policy protecting her gorgeous gams for a half million dollars.

MELODIE JOHNSON played an early-west saloon entertainer in a co-star role with Jack Lord and James Farentino in Universal's *The Ride to Hangman's Tree.*

230

A rare leg-art shot of GRACE KELLY, now Princess Grace of Monaco. Before marriage to Prince Rainier, she won an Oscar for her stunning performance in *The Country Girl*.

The shapely British beauty JOAN COLLINS posed prettily for her role in MGM's *The Opposite Sex*. She recently wrote an autobiography, filled with romances and boudoir romps, which was published in England, but Joan withdrew United States printing to avoid unwittingly hurting American friends.

The comely British actress DIANA RIGG had hit stardom with her role on TV in the popular series *The Avengers*. She also cavorted with James Bond in the film *On Her Majesty's Secret Service*.

JULIET PROWSE, the dancing star, struck a "Betty Grable" pose for a publicity photo heralding her 1971 supper-club act at Las Vegas' Desert Inn.

PIA LINDSTROM, the daughter of Ingrid Bergman, experienced a brief and undistinguished screen career. Today she is a television news reporter.

Among DOROTHY PROVINE's movie credits, such as the hits *It's a Mad, Mad, Mad, Mad World* and *The Great Race*, was a movie called *The Thirty Foot Bride of Candy Rock.*

PATTY DUKE's leg-art pose is keyed to an acting characterization. As a teenager she won an Oscar for *The Miracle Worker.* Married to John Astin, she currently appears on screen as Patty Duke Astin.

233

JULIE CHRISTIE won an Oscar for *Darling* and was nominated for her performance in *McCabe and Mrs. Miller*.

The attractive screen star Diahann Carroll won an Academy Award nomination for her fine performance in *Claudine*. Among her other films: *Carmen Jones, Porgy and Bess, Paris Blues,* and *Hurry Sundown.*

Gina Lollobrigida displays great legs as a circus acrobat in *Trapeze*. Today she gains additional fame as a professional photographer.

When it comes to leg competition among Hollywood's beauties, Angie Dickinson is a finalist. Her popularity zoomed when she played the title role in the hit TV series *Policewoman.*

The tempting Parisienne MYLENE DEMONGEOT struck this come-hither pose while on oceanic location for her co-starring role with Van Heflin and Charles Laughton in the World War II suspense drama *Under Ten Flags*.

ANGIE DICKINSON.

A unique pose by the fine dramatic actress FAYE DUNAWAY, who played a fashion model in *Puzzle of a Downfall Child* and a fashion photographer in *The Eyes of Laura Mars*. Faye won an Oscar for her dynamic role in Paddy Chayefsky's *Network*.

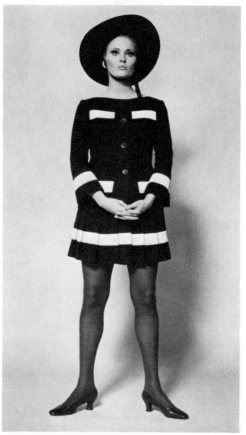

236

TINA LOUISE danced on Broadway in *Lil Abner* and made a delightful movie debut as a sexy southern bell in *God's Little Acre*.

ANN-MARGRET, as she appeared in a musical number for MGM's *Viva Las Vegas* with Elvis Presley.

SUE LYON popularized the word nymphet, when she portrayed that characterization opposite James Mason in her film debut title role of *Lolita*.

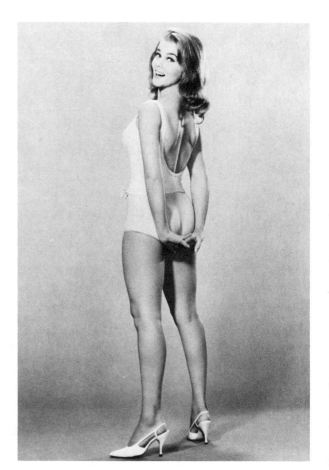

ANN-MARGRET strikes the famous Grable pose. She went to the same high school as Rock Hudson.

ELIZABETH MONTGOMERY, daughter of one of the screen's greatest stars, Robert Montgomery, first achieved prominence with the popular TV series *Bewitched*.

LIZA MINNELLI was twenty and portraying Albert Finney's secretary in Universal's *Charlie Bubbles* when this picture was taken.

SHARON TATE.

239

Among Raquel Welch's many films were *One Million Years B.C.*, *Bandolero*, *Myra Breckenridge*, *Kansas City Bomber*, *The Four Musketeers*, and *Mother, Jugs and Speed*.

A star in France before coming to the United States and 20th Century-Fox, Annabella appeared in *The Baroness and the Butler*. She was later to become Mrs. Tyrone Power. Until her death in 1979, she divided her time between an apartment in Paris and a farm in the French Pyrenees.

Ursula Andress, a native of Switzerland, had the perfect measurements for a James Bond film. She displayed her curves in two Bond adventures, *Dr. No* and *Casino Royale*.

Another *eye-filling* cinema sexpot Senta Berger hails from Germany.

While playing the title role in Ross Hunter's production of *Thoroughly Modern Millie*, Julie Andrews strikes the same classic shipboard pose that years earlier inspired a new word in the English language—*cheesecake*.

The celebrated TV comedienne CAROL BURNETT parodies a leg-art pose at a Hollywood social event.

The attractive British actress SAMANTHA EGGAR is here shown sharing her gorgeous gams with the signs of the Zodiac. She was an Oscar nominee for her role in *The Collector*.

242

The British beauty CARROLL BAKER achieved full stardom in the title role of *Baby Doll*, which won her an Oscar nomination. She later portrayed Jean Harlow in a film.

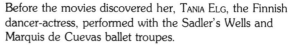

Barbara Eden added a generous portion of leg art to the TV tube as the star of *I Dream of Jeanie*.

Before the movies discovered her, Tania Elg, the Finnish dancer-actress, performed with the Sadler's Wells and Marquis de Cuevas ballet troupes.

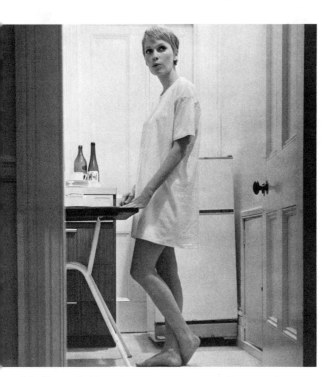

Mia Farrow's biggest screen success was *Rosemary's Baby*. Most of her early personal publicity stemmed from her marriage to Frank Sinatra.

Many film critics consider JANE FONDA the number-one dramatic actress of the screen. Hank Fonda's daughter is also extremely outspoken on the political scene. Jane won Oscars for her powerful performances in *Klute* and *Coming Home.* She is seen here in an earlier film, *Walk on the Wild Side.*

ELKE SOMMER's delightful figure has been featured prominently in many movies. Here she hides behind a wardrobe of soap bubbles in a scene in Universal's *The Art of Love.*

NANCY SINATRA poses to publicize MGM's *Speedway.*

244

CORINNE CALVET came to Hollywood from her native France and was labeled a cinema sexpot—"the new Hayworth."

YVETTE MIMIEUX was born in Los Angeles and graduated from Hollywood High School.

STELLA STEVENS hails from Hot Coffee, Mississippi.

245

"THOU SHALT NOT"
1 LAW DEFEATED
2 INSIDE OF THIGH
3 LACE LINGERIE
4 DEAD MAN
5 NARCOTICS
6 DRINKING
7 EXPOSED BOSOM
8 GAMBLING
9 POINTING GUN
10 TOMMY GUN

An enterprising photographer posed this shot to break every one of THE TEN COMMANDMENTS OF MOVIE CENSORSHIP dictated by the movie industry's self-governing censorship regulations enforced by the Hays Office.

DEBBIE REYNOLDS.

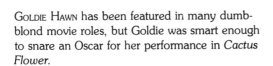

GOLDIE HAWN has been featured in many dumb-blond movie roles, but Goldie was smart enough to snare an Oscar for her performance in *Cactus Flower*.

Sophia Loren has been a popular international screen star for more than twenty-five years. She is still one of the great cinema beauties.

Six dancing lovelies recruited by movie choreographer Bobby Connolly to swing a mean bolero in Mervyn LeRoy's Warner Bros. film *The King and the Chorus Girl* which starred Fernand Gravet and Joan Blondell.

A dream shot for leg-art lovers as ALICE WHITE and Chester
Morris play a scene for *Playing Around*. The year is 1930.

250

RITA LA ROY.

GLORIA SWANSON went on to become a major star, but here she is hamming it up as a Sennett bathing beauty with another of the Sennet sweeties.

BEAUTY CONTEST: Mack Sennett staged a competiton among swimsuited damsels on the beach at Venice, California, in 1917. Sennett bathing beauties won first, second, and third prizes. Here is that year's lineup, with rising young star MARIE PREVOST fifth from the left.

Mack Sennett's Bathing Beauties

The screen's king of comedy, Mack Sennett, popularized the bathing beauty as a ploy to get his famous Keystone Kops more newspaper publicity. No one wanted to run a photo of Ben Turpin's crossed eyes, but with a shapely doll in a swimsuit linking her arm with Ben's, newspaper editors had a change of heart. From that time on, the crazy Kops shared publicity honors with pretty girls.

253

Mack Sennett bathing beauty MYRTLE CORY.

This rare leg-art photo of JOAN CRAWFORD in the twenties is a collector's item.

Not all the Sennett beauties were confined to beaches. EVELYN FRANCISCO was a 1925 selection of Sennett's as a star-to-be. He described her as "twenty, blue-eyed, blond. and bobbed."

And Other Beauties

THE MARION MORGAN DANCERS during filming of an early
Metropolitan movie entitled *Almost a Lady*.

A quintet of screen lovelies, left to right: ELEANOR BAILEY, ROSALIE ROY, ANN INGRAHAM, LOIS LACY, and PEGGY GROVE.

ANN SHERIDAN, center, is surrounded by Warner Bros.' *Navy Blues* Sextet, who toured the nation to publicize the film.

256

After Mack Sennett enjoyed promotional success with his bathing beauties, other movie studios followed suit. Here are the Fox Sunshine Girls at Fox Films.

This lineup of girls from 20th Century-Fox's *Girls' Dormitory,* starring Simone Simon, is unusual because in the movie they neither sang nor danced. Composed mainly of studio stock girls of that day, the roster included, left to right: Lynne Berkeley, Lynn Bari, June Storey, Julie Cabanne, Esther Brodelet, Mary Blackwood, and Madelon Earle.

257

This showgirl quartet appeared in MGM's movie *The Way of a Girl,* which starred Eleanor Boardman and Matt Moore.

Student Tour was a low-budget MGM musical of 1934, and one of the girls in the film was destined for great screen heights. On the right—BETTY GRABLE.

Flanked by two unidentified beach beauties, VERA REYNOLDS starred for Cecil B. De Mille in three 1924–25 films, *Feet of Clay, The Golden Bed,* and *The Road to Yesterday.*

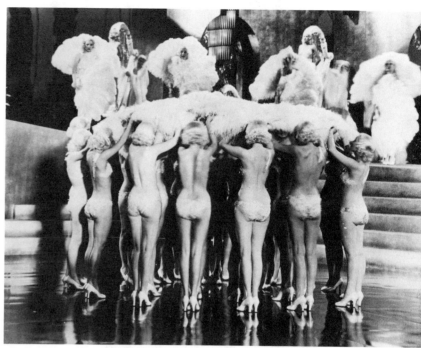

An elaborate musical number staged by Busby Berkeley for the big musical *Fashions of 1934*.

259

An unusual leg-art trio, left to right: MARIE DRESSLER, BESSIE LOVE, and POLLY MORAN.

MARI BLANCHARD as she appeared in Universal's *Veils of Bagdad.*

LAURA LEE, a leading lady of the thirties, eventually graduated to character roles.

260

MAMIE VAN DOREN.

The James Bond girls have always been
sultry sexpots, and MARTINE BESWICK, who
appeared with Sean Connery in
Thunderball, was no exception.

BETTY COMPSON.

King Kong's leading lady FAY WRAY in the
original version of the famed screen thriller.
Fay is shown here in a pose for *King Kong*
known in those days as advertising art.

262

Clara Bow in a 1928 pose.

AGNES AYRES.

BILLIE DOVE.

CONSTANCE BENNETT in a scene with Charlie Murray.

LILY PONS in a jungle scene for a movie called *Hitting a New High*.

MAE WEST.

DOROTHY BURGESS shown here in *The Bird of Flame* (1930).

ANN BLYTH.

ANNA HELD, the great Ziegfeld star, ma[de] the milk bath famous. She starred on [the] screen in 1916 in *Madame la Presiden[t].* Many years later Luise Rainer won an Oscar for her portrayal of Held in *The Great Ziegfeld.*

Noel Francis played a gambling-hall siren in First National's *Smart Money,* starring Edward G. Robinson.

Sisters G identified themselves with only their last initial. Their names were Eleanor and Carla Gutohrlen.

Lynn Browning.

Harriet Hilliard.

HEDY LAMARR in a starring role with John Hodiak in MGM's *Visa*. She portrayed a Cuban nightclub entertainer.

MARGARET LIVINGSTON.

COLLEEN MOORE.

BETTY GRABLE in a starring role with Marge and Gower Champion and Jack Lemmon in the Columbia musical *Three for the Show*.

269

ROSITA MORENO, in a Paramount publicity shot captioned "At Home with Rosita Moreno."

VIOLET TILLIE used this photo to attract talent scouts. On the back she had written her statistics: "Height, 5 ft. 3 in.—Weight, 120 lb.—Large brown eyes, long black lashes, lovely narrow eyebrows—black long hair—age 19 next birthday—light comp.—dancer, stay-at-home—I forgot to put age on other photo—not married, never been married."

CURLS MASON, An early-day stripteuse at the Los Angeles Burbank burlesque theater.

MARY MILES MINTER.

GINGER ROGERS.

Here's an early LORETTA YOUNG as one of Santa's helpers.

This publicity photo of BEBE DANIELS was shot in 1915.

271

NORMA SHEARER.

HELENE COSTELLO, a leading lady of the twenties, hailed from a famous acting family that included her sister Dolores and her father, Maurice.

HELEN TWELVETREES.

MOLLY McGOWAN in a very risque shot for its day.

The twin DOLLY SISTERS, Jenny and Rosie, starred on screen in 1918 in *The Million Dollar Dollies.* Many years later, their lives were put on screen with Betty Grable and June Haver playing the title roles.

The French actress ANNIE GIRARDOT in her role as an amoral woman in *Vice and Virtue*, directed by Roger Vadim and also starring Catherine Deneuve, Robert Hossein, and O. E. Hasse.

VIVIANE VENTURA was a bathing beauty who went near the water. Viviane strikes a publicity pose during filming of *A High Wind in Jamaica*.

STEPHANIE POWERS in a provocative scene from the 1965 Columbia film *Love Has Many Faces*.

LILY DAMITA.

SARI MARITZA.

ELKE SOMMER.

The Italian actress SILVIA MONTI was appearing with David
Niven, Jean-Paul Belmondo, Eli Wallach, and Bourvil in
the French film *The Brain* when this was taken.

GALE SONDERGAARD modeling a
bathing suit she wore for her role in
Paramount's *Never Say Die*.

277

The famous haystack shot that made JANE RUSSELL a star before she ever got on the screen in *The Outlaw*. While Howard Hughes withheld the film's release for two years, his publicity mill soon made the world realize that Russell was special.

VERA MILES.

Barbra Streisand, giving her impression of Baby Snooks during her Oscar-winning performance as Fanny Brice in *Funny Girl*.

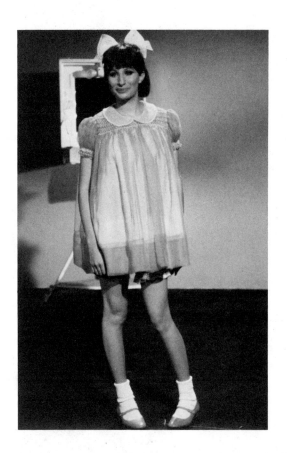

Conchita Montenegro, shown here in a New Year's pose.

Jo Ann Pflug.

ADELE JERGENS, performin...
number for Columbia's
Love.

RAQUEL WELCH.

JEAN ROGERS's film career began in the
thirties. If Jean was not appearing in
serials she was in a series, such as *Flash
Gordon, Ace Drummond, Mr. Moto,
The Cisco Kid, Charlie Chan, Dr.
Kildare,* or *Maisie.*

MARIE WINDSOR is today happily married to wealthy Beverly Hills realtor Jack Hupp. She is also a prominent movietown hostess, and active in Screen Actors Guild affairs.

INDEX

Adams, Julie, 207
Adams, Abigail, 207
Adams, Neile, 214
Adrian, Iris, 117
Alcorn, Olive Ann, 88
Allen, Judith, 208
Allison, May, 40
Allwyn, Astrid, 146
Ames, Adrienne, 165
Anderson, Dusty, 214
Andress, Ursula, 241
Andrews, Julie, 241
Angel, Heather, 105
Annabella, 240
Ann-Margret, 238
Aquanetta, 215
Arthur, Jean, 107
Astin, Patty Duke, 233
Astor, Mary, 107
Ayres, Agnes, 29, 264

Bacall, Lauren, 71
Bailey, Eleanor, 256
Baker, Carroll, 242
Ball, Lucille, 119
Bancroft, Anne, 188
Bara, Theda, 13
Bardot, Brigitte, 27
Bari, Lynn, 257
Barnes, Binnie, 144
Barrett, Judith, 189
Barrie, Wendy, 178
Bates, Barbara, 187
Belita, 192
Bellamy, Madge, 117, 138
Bennett, Constance, 110, 264
Bennett, Joan, 110
Bergen, Polly, 188

Berger, Senta, 241
Bergman, Ingrid, 178
Berkeley, Lynne, 257
Beswick, Martine, 262
Bettis, Valerie, 191
Bishop, Julie, 117, 137
Blackwood, Mary, 257
Blanchard, Mari, 180
Blane, Sally, 139
Blondell, Gloria, 136
Blondell, Joan, 23
Blyth, Ann, 136, 266
Blythe, Betty, 37
Boardman, Eleanor, 85
Booth, Edwina, 90
Borden, Olive, 101
Borg, Veda Ann, 144
Bow, Clara, 94, 263
Bowe, Rosemarie, 190
Bradley, Grace, 190
Brent, Evelyn, 103
Brian, Mary, 137
Brice, Fanny, 98
Britt, May, 213
Britton, Mozelle, 142
Broadhurst, Ethel, 12
Brooks, Leslie, 182
Brooks, Louise, 117
Brown, Vanessa, 179
Browning, Lynn, 268
Bruce, Virginia, 118
Burgess, Dorothy, 177, 266
Burke, Kathleen, 143
Burnett, Carol, 242

Cabanne, Julie, 257
Calvet, Corinne, 245
Carlisle, Kitty, 206

Carlisle, Mary, 141
Carol, Sue, 87
Caron, Leslie, 203
Carroll, Diahann, 235
Carroll, Georgia, 167
Carroll, Nancy, 112, 141
Carter, Janis, 205
Castle, Peggie, 203
Caulfield, Joan, 204
Chadwick, Helene, 42
Charisse, Cyd, 202
Chatterton, Ruth, 91
Chevret, Lita, 140
Christie, Julie, 234
Churchill, Marguerite, 166
Clark, Mae, 92
Clifford, Ruth, 87
Clooney, Rosemary, 206
Clyde, June, 166
Colbert, Claudette, 141
Colby, Anita, 71
Collins, Joan, 232
Compson, Betty, 39, 262
Compton, Juliette, 140
Conway, Edna, 110
Coonan, Dorothy, 116
Cory, Myrtle, 254
Costello, Dolores, 90
Costello, Helene, 90, 272
Craig, Yvonne, 193
Crawford, Joan, 102, 254
Crawford, Kathryn, 141

Dagover, Lil, 145
Dahl, Arlene, 210
Dale, Virginia, 186
Dalton, Dorothy, 37
Damita, Lily, 116, 275

Dana, Viola, 51
Daniels, Bebe, 89, 271
Darcel, Denise, 209
Darnell, Linda, 168
Davies, Marion, 23, 89
Davis, Bette, 144
D'Avril, Yola, 95, 110
Day, Doris, 179
Day, Laraine, 184
Day, Marcelline, 109
Deane, Priscilla, 38
De Camp, Rosemary, 140
De Carlo, Yvonne, 166
Dee, Sandra, 186
De Haven, Gloria, 143
De Havilland, Olivia, 112
Dell, Claudia, 108, 145
Dell, Myrna, 168
Del Rio, Dolores, 145
Delroy, Irene, 110
Demongeot, Mylene, 236
Dempster, Carol, 89
Devore, Dorothy, 94
Dickinson, Angie, 235, 236
Dietrich, Marlene, 72, 116
Dolly Sisters, 273
Domergue, Faith, 178
Donahue, Elinor, 179
Donnell, Jeff, 187
Donnelly, Ruth, 108
Dore, Nadine, 146
Dors, Diana, 211
D'Orsay, Fifi, 105
Dove, Billie, 42, 264
Drake, Frances, 140
Dressler, Marie, 260
Drew, Ellen, 209
Duke, Patty, 233
Duna, Steffi, 181
Dunaway, Faye, 236
Dunbar, Dixie, 165
Duncan, Mary, 98
Durbin, Deanna, 140

Earle, Madelon, 257
Eden, Barbara, 243
Eggar, Samantha, 242
Eilers, Sally, 138
Ekberg, Anita, 212
Elg, Tania, 243
Ellis, Patricia, 213

Fabray, Nanette, 168

Faire, Virginia Brown, 94
Falkenburg, Jinx, 17
Farmer, Frances, 138
Farrell, Glenda, 138
Farrow, Mia, 243
Faye, Alice, 116, 173
Fazenda, Louise, 89
Field, Virginia, 169
Fitzgerald, Geraldine, 142
Fleming, Rhonda, 171
Fonda, Jane, 244
Fontaine, Joan, 115
Foster, Susanna, 168
Fox, Sidney, 169
Fox Sunshine Girls, 257
Francis, Anne, 114, 169
Francis, Kay, 107
Francis, Noel, 108, 268
Francisco, Evelyn, 254
Franklin, Louise, 201
Frazee, Jane, 169
Fulton, Joan, 168

Gabor, Eva, 150
Gabor, Magda, 150
Gabor, Zsa Zsa, 150
Gam, Rita, 127
Garbo, Greta, 96
Gardner, Ava, 149
Garson, Greer, 133
Gaynor, Janet, 95
Gaynor, Mitzi, 116
Geraghty, Carmelita, 85
Gilbert, Jane, 126
Girardot, Annie, 274
Gish, Dorothy, 36
Gish, Lillian, 36
Goddard, Paulette, 162
Grable, Betty, 31, 79, 115, 258, 269
Grahame, Gloria, 146
Grahame, Margot, 127
Granger, Dorothy, 159
Granville, Bonita, 134
Gray, Dolores, 159
Gray, Gilda, 98
Grayson, Kathryn, 134
Green, Mitzi, 134
Grey, Virginia, 134
Griffith, Corinne, 46
Grove, Peggy, 256

Hale, Barbara, 229

Halsey, Mary Jane, 126
Hammond, Harriet, 80
Hampton, Hope, 94
Hansen, Juanita, 84
Harlow, Jean, 18, 56, 114
Harvey, Lilian, 114
Haver, June, 148, 229
Havoc, June, 158
Hawley, Wanda, 84
Hawn, Goldie, 247
Hayes, Allison, 150
Hayward, Susan, 162
Hayworth, Rita, 20, 62
Held, Anna, 267
Henie, Sonja, 148
Hepburn, Katharine, 147
Hervey, Irene, 103
Hill, Doris, 135
Hilliard, Harriet, 104, 268
Holliday, Judy, 148
Holm, Eleanor, 126
Hopkins, Miriam, 135
Horne, Lena, 158
Hudson, Rochelle, 83
Hume, Benita, 105, 106
Hunt, Eleanor, 104
Hunt, Marsha, 159
Hussey, Ruth, 126
Hutton, Betty, 161
Hyams, Leila, 156
Hyer, Martha, 228

Inescort, Frieda, 133
Ingraham, Ann, 256

James, Claire, 119
James, Lois, 120
Jergens, Adele, 227, 280
Johnson, Melodie, 230
Johnson, Rita, 151
Jones, Carolyn, 220
Jones, Shirley, 153
Judge, Arlene, 120

Keeler, Ruby, 24
Kellerman, Annette, 14
Kelly, Grace, 231
Kelly, Nancy, 105
Kendall, Kay, 218
Kerr, Deborah, 160
Keyes, Evelyn, 163
King, Ruth, 104
Knight, June, 104

Kwan, Nancy, 215

Lacy, Lois, 256
Lake, Veronica, 19, 113
LaMarr, Barbara, 86
Lamarr, Hedy, 99, 269
Lamour, Dorothy, 22, 65
Lamphier, Fay, 95
Lanchester, Elsa, 137
Landis, Carole, 25, 68
Lane, Abbe, 161
Lane, Priscilla, 129
Lane, Rosemary, 129
Lange, Hope, 219
Lansbury, Angela, 165
Lansing, Joi, 156
LaPlante, Laura, 95
LaRoy, Rita, 100, 251
Laurie, Piper, 160
Lawford, Betty, 128
Lawrence, Barbara, 219
Lawson, Patricia, 129
Lee, Dixie, 108
Lee, Gwen, 99
Lee, Gypsy Rose, 130
Lee, Laura, 127
Lee, Lila, 104
Leeds, Andrea, 160
Leigh, Janet, 217
Leslie, Joan, 130
Lewis, Diana, 127
Lightner, Winnie, 96
Lindsay, Lois, 130
Lindsay, Margaret, 129
Lindstrom, Pia, 233
Livingston, Margaret, 95, 269
Loff, Jeanette, 129
Lollobrigida, Gina, 235
Lombard, Carole, 30, 93
Loraine, Lillian, 94
Loren, Sophia, 248
Louise, Anita, 99
Louise, Tina, 237
Love, Bessie, 51, 260
Loy, Myrna, 96
Lupino, Ida, 113
Lyon, Sue, 238

McAvoy, May, 101
McCambridge, Mercedes, 124
McDonald, Grace, 157
McDonald, Marie, 25, 69
McGowan, Molly, 272

MacDonald, Jeanette, 136
Mackaill, Dorothy, 16, 102
MacLaine, Shirley, 221
Main, Marjorie, 125
Malone, Dorothy, 185
Mansfield, Jayne, 153
Maple, Christine, 125
Marion Morgan Dancers, 255
Maris, Mona, 125
Maritza, Sari, 136, 276
Marsh, Mae, 48
Marsh, Marian, 124
Mason, Curls, 270
Martin, Marion, 155
Martin, Mary, 165
Martinelli, Elsa, 217
Mason, Shirley, 51
Massey, Ilona, 124
Matthews, Jessie, 135
Maxwell, Marilyn, 157
Mayo, Virginia, 112, 113
Merman, Ethel, 101
Meyers, Carmel, 92
Michael, Gertrude, 155
Miles, Vera, 158, 278
Miller, Ann, 156
Miller, Marilyn, 92
Miller, Patsy Ruth, 101, 102
Mimieux, Yvette, 245
Minnelli, Liza, 239
Minter, Mary Miles, 48, 271
Miranda, Carmen, 158
Mistinguette, 75
Monroe, Marilyn, 26, 76
Montenegro, Conchita, 125, 279
Montevecchi, Liliane, 216
Montez, Maria, 124
Montgomery, Elizabeth, 239
Monti, Silvia, 277
Moore, Colleen, 93, 269
Moore, Constance, 157
Moore, Mary Tyler, 216
Moore, Terry, 222
Moorehead, Natalie, 119
Moran, Polly, 260
Moreno, Rita, 157
Moreno, Rosita, 270
Morgan, Dolores, 124
Morley, Karen, 135
Movita, 220
Murray, Mae, 16

Nazimova, Alla, 43

Neagle, Anna, 106
Nelson, Lori, 196
Newmar, Julie, 223
Nichols, Barbara, 172
Niesen, Gertrude, 142
Nixon, Marian, 106
Nolan, Mary, 107
Normand, Mabel, 14, 58
Novak, Eva, 87
Novak, Kim, 197

Oberon, Merle, 164
O'Hara, Maureen, 121
O'Sullivan, Maureen, 109, 131

Page, Anita, 103
Page, Geraldine, 177
Paget, Debra, 152
Paige, Janis, 122
Palmer, Betsy, 222
Parker, Jean, 109, 122
Parrish, Helen, 121
Patten, Luana, 152
Pennington, Ann, 17
Pepper, Barbara, 120
Perdue, Derelys, 86
Peters, Jean, 193
Pflug, Jo Ann, 195, 279
Piazza, Marguerite, 146
Pickford, Mary, 17, 35
Pons, Lily, 122, 264
Powell, Eleanor, 148
Powell, Jane, 152
Powers, Stephanie, 274
Pretty, Arlene, 87
Prevost, Marie, 32
Provine, Dorothy, 233
Prowse, Juliet, 232

Raines, Ella, 177
Ralston, Esther, 143
Ralston, Vera Hruba, 161
Rambeau, Marjorie, 91
Rand, Sally, 10
Raye, Martha, 142
Reed, Donna, 144
Revier, Dorothy, 107
Reynolds, Debbie, 176, 247
Reynolds, Vera, 258
Rigg, Diana, 232
Riordan, Marjorie, 195
Robbins, Gale, 196
Rogers, Ginger, 143, 271

Rogers, Jean, 281
Roland, Ruth, 43
Roman, Ruth, 142
Roth, Lillian, 112
Roy, Rosalie, 183, 256
Rush, Barbara, 198
Russell, Connie, 195
Russell, Jane, 194, 278
Russell, Rosalind, 175

Saint, Eva Marie, 173
St. Cyr, Lili, 154
St. John, Betta, 171
St. John, Jill, 201
Savage, Ann, 175
Sebastian, Dorothy, 83
Segal, Vivienne, 91
Sennett, Mack, Bathing Beauties,
    50
Seymour, Clarine, 15
Shaw, Wini, 120
Shearer, Norma, 82, 271
Sheridan, Ann, 22, 65, 256
Shirley, Anne, 108, 111
Shore, Dinah, 199
Short, Gertrude, 93
Simon, Simone, 173, 257
Sinatra, Nancy, 244
Sisters G, 105, 268
Smith, Alexis, 174
Sommer, Elke, 244, 277
Sondergaard, Gale, 174, 277
Sothern, Ann, 99, 131
Stanwyck, Barbara, 82
Starke, Pauline, 92
Sterling, Jan, 199

Stevens, Risë, 131
Stevens, Stella, 245
Stevenson, Venetia, 200
Stewart, Elaine, 198
Storey, June, 257
Storm, Gale, 182
Streisand, Barbra, 279
Stuart, Gloria, 162
Swanson, Gloria, 44, 253
Swarthout, Gladys, 131
Sweet, Blanche, 28

Talmadge, Norma, 43
Tashman, Lilyan, 123
Taylor, Elizabeth, 101
Temple, Shirley, 130
Ten Commandments of Movie
    Censorship, 246
Terry, Ruth, 129
Terry, Sheila, 102
Tillie, Violet, 270
Tobin, Genevieve, 103
Todd, Thelma, 105
Torres, Nancy, 98
Totter, Audrey, 113
Toumanova, Tamara, 123
Tovar, Lupita, 123
Towers, Constance, 215
Towne, Rosella, 162
Trevor, Claire, 123
Turner, Lana, 21, 63
Twelvetrees, Helen, 91, 272

Van Doren, Mamie, 224, 261
Vanity Fair Maids, 52, 55
Vargas, Amelita, 153
Vaughn, Alberta, 85

Velez, Lupe, 121
Ventura, Viviane, 274
Vera-Ellen, 185
Verdon, Gwen, 226
Verdugo, Elena, 152
Vickers, Martha, 152
Vitale, Milly, 224

Walker, Helen, 151
Welch, Raquel, 240, 281
West, Mae, 97, 265
Westcott, Helen, 151
Whelan, Arlene, 151
White, Alice, 106, 111, 250
Whitney, Eleanore, 119
Williams, Cara, 120
Williams, Chili, 28
Williams, Edy, 225
Williams, Esther, 151
Williams, Kay, 119
Wilson, Marie, 132
Windsor, Claire, 45
Windsor, Marie, 282
Wing, Toby, 104
Winters, Shelley, 147
Withers, Jane, 111
Wong, Anna May, 90
Wood, Natalie, 225
Woodbury, Joan, 225
Woodward, Joanne, 228
Wray, Fay, 111, 262
Wyman, Jane, 133

Young, Loretta, 132, 271

Zorina, Vera, 132